D0284976

THE ARTICLES OF BUSINESS

Books by Vivian Kistler

Library of Professional Picture Framing
Vol I Picture Framing
Vol II Mat Cutting & Decoration
Vol III Framing Needlework
Object Box Framing
Framer's Work Scheduling Book
Business Forms for Galleries and Frameshops

Videos by Vivian Kistler

Basic Picture Framing
Mat Cutting & Decoration
Framing Needlework
Conservation Framing
Color Selection in Matting

THE ARTICLES OF BUSINESS

for the Framing & Art Trade

An anthology of business articles
by Vivian Carli Kistler

Originally published in
DECOR Magazine
1981 to 1993
Revised and Updated

Foreword by Alice C. Gibson

COLUMBA PUBLISHING COMPANY
Akron, Ohio

The Articles of Business
by Vivian C. Kistler

Published by Columba Publishing Company
Akron, Ohio

Printed & Manufactured in the United States of America
ISBN 0–938655–28–0
10 9 8 7 6 5 4 3 2

Copy Editors:
Elizabeth A. Leahy
Carli Kistler Miller

To my mentor, my mother

C. Isabella Cutini Carli

1910 – 1990

ACKNOWLEDGMENTS

Long before trade associations and conventions, *DECOR* magazine provided the art and framing industry with business news and education. Framers and gallery owners could depend on their monthly lessons on matters of mats and mounting. The instruction has proven invaluable.

The opportunity to write for the magazine, to speak at trade shows and to work with extraordinary editors helped me develop as a professional. Thanks to Alice Curless Gibson for her flexible deadlines, William G. Cotner for his marketing savvy, Shelia Flanagan Stock for hanging up my dangling participles, and William M. Humberg for dedicating so much of the magazine to the picture framing industry.

Thanks to my colleague Robert Mayfield who continues to teach me the value of pricing. He co–authored chapter 6, *Pricing*. I am grateful to James Burke for initiating the pricing formula. And to my colleague William Parker for defining ratios and the revised and updated version of chapter 3, *Financial Statements.*

A special thank you to commercial loan officer, Susan Snodgrass Ernst for her continuing interest in my businesses and her assistance with questions on bank loans on pages 146 to 148.

The U.S. Small Business Administration and the University of Akron, Akron, Ohio for information, assistance and the opportunity to teach.

Contents

Foreword xi

I. *General Business*

1	Starting a Frame Shop or Gallery	3
2	Bookkeeping & Accounting	7
3	Financial Statements	11
4	The Budget: A Guide to Cash Control	17
5	Credit Terms from Suppliers	21

II. *Management*

6	Pricing the Custom Product	27
7	Customer Service	35
8	Time Management	41
9	Planning for Growth	45
10	Economic Survival	51

III. *Advertising*

11	Advertising	61
12	Developing A Plan	65

IV. *Commercial Sales*

13	Corporate Sales	71
14	Volume Framing	75
15	Leasing Framed Artwork	79
16	Credit Department	83

V. Questions & Answers

17	General Business	89
	Personnel	94
	Management	98
	Production	101
	Gallery	103
	Merchandising	114
	Customer Relations	123
	Location	132
	Advertising	135
	Corporate Sales	139
	Finance	146
	Accounting	150
	Pricing	154
Index		159
Appendix		167

Foreword

Vivian Kistler, CPF, first appeared on the pages of *DECOR* in late 1979; in the spring of the next year, she was back, posing with Pierrot, a 12–foot marionette that was the "star" of her gallery window display.

Pierrot served as the mascot and a primary means of promotion at Kistler Art and Frame in Akron, Ohio, for several years. As a promotion effort, he served the shop well. He cost almost nothing — being made from leftover mailing tubes, plaster of Paris and cheesecloth — and he was fun. He beckoned customers from the window in a variety of poses, and he promoted the shop by appearing in holiday parades.

Pierrot symbolized the spirit of Kistler Art and Frame. Retailing is a serious business — if one hopes to earn a living at it — but it can also be fun.

For example, Vivian was discussing at a seminar in Milwaukee various kinds of frame shop equipment. She explained to students the advantages and disadvantages of each, but in her own unmatchable style of communication. About a particular brand of mat cutter, Vivian said, "It's kind of like my ex–husband. It's good looking, but it doesn't work."

Over the years, we have heard most of Vivian's favorite stories:

· the one about the sports car bumper she framed — all that was left from the customer's expensive hobby after the accident . . .

· the one about her Italian Mother who spoke about "Sal" to customers when referring to Salvador Dali . . .

· the one about the Pope's signature on the damaged parchment . . .

· the one about the delivery truck driver who used a board with stretched needleart on it to haul mat boards across a puddle . . .

· the one about the stuffed cat in the shadow box frame . . .

· the one . . . the one . . . the one . . .

The point is, in more than 20 years of operating a gallery and frame shop, Vivian has been there. It's what makes her advice so noteworthy and useful. Her willingness to share such experiences — and how she solved them — has endeared her to framers, gallery owners, students and friends.

As endearing as all this is, however, Vivian realized early in her career as a retailer that solving day–to–day problems was not enough if she hoped to survive and grow. As a former artist and art teacher, she discovered quickly that she was woefully inadequate when it came to running a business.

"My lack of business training became an annoying handicap," she said. "I didn't understand the statements my accountants were giving me. I didn't even know the right questions to ask."

Beginning with business courses at Wharton School of Business and continuing with seminars and readings, Vivian learned to understand her business and also became an avid student of the art and framing industry as a whole. Over the years, the attention she devoted to the industry has made her an expert in retail operations; in framing techniques, supplies and equipment; and in frame shop and gallery management.

As a consultant to other gallery owners, she has seen a myriad of problems and has helped to find solutions. As a consultant to industry suppliers, she has helped those suppliers "connect" to the retail customer, devising and offering products that help them solve problems. As a speaker, teacher, and writer, she has shared with the industry problems and solutions from both sides through the pages of *DECOR*.

Vivian has served on our panel of "Ask the Experts" inviting readers to send in different questions. She also has written numerous feature articles on a wide variety of topics from advertising, to pricing, to personnel management, to customer service, to color and design trends. She is a regular speaker at our ABC Show Learning Center seminar programs, and is a part of our *DECOR* Workshop faculty.

As the owner of Columba Publishing Company, Vivian has published a series of her own books and videotapes on framing and has produced a number of books and videotapes by other industry experts as well.

She is an outspoken proponent for increasing the level of professionalism among art dealers and framers. She was among the first framers to take and pass her test to become a Certified Picture Framer, and proudly wears the CPF after her name.

We are justifiably proud of our relationship with Vivian Kistler, CPF, and are pleased to have her present this collection of her writings from the pages of *DECOR*.

Alice C. Gibson, CPF
Editor
DECOR

The Articles of Business

Part I

General Business

1

Starting a Frame Shop or Gallery

Before opening a business you need to do a little groundwork. You've probably spent the last three months buying equipment, inventory, displays, and tools; renting a store space; and choosing paint and carpeting! Now you need to plan *who* will buy, *when* they will buy, and *how much* they will buy.

Get a pencil and paper (go on — this will only take a few minutes), and write your answers to the following questions. Yes, I want you to write them down. There may be a pop quiz at the end of this chapter, and I want you to be prepared.

- What kind of business are you really in?
- What goods and services will you provide?
- Where is your market?
- Who will buy?
- When and why will they buy?
- What will be your sales strategy?

Easy, right? On what did you base your answers? Common sense? An educated guess? Market research? BINGO! Market research is not out of the reach of the small–business person. At least, give me a chance to explain. Market research is for the mom–and–pop shop as well as the million dollar gallery and you can do it yourself.

What Is Market Research?

The term market research covers a broad range of activities. It encompasses the gathering and analyzing of facts relevant to problems arising during the transfer and sale of goods and services. Thus, market research can be used to study and improve almost any aspect of a firm's operation, including location, sales, advertising, display, image, packaging, transportation, and customer satisfaction.

Look at the kind of information you should seek. You need to know the trading area and its traffic pattern. The customer profile — age, sex, occupation, income, shopping habits, social standing — is very important. So, too, are types of surrounding business, their hours, yearly sales, advertising practices, and general appeal.

Where do you find this information? The following information is available at little or no cost. It will give you a lot about which to think. Just add common sense and personal judgment to all the facts, and you'll be prepared for business.

1. The local chamber of commerce should be able to furnish you with traffic counts and other data.
2. The main library in your city or town has a wealth of information in the business and commerce section. You won't need a library card, but you may need money for the photocopier.
3. The market research department of the local newspaper has detailed information about the buying practices of its readers, including their income, buying frequency, where they buy, and on what they spend their money.
4. Check the phone book under "Government Offices–Federal" or the main branch of a public library for information from the most current census.
5. National and regional industry surveys in trade publications are available. *DECOR*'s annual forecast (January issue) and pricing (July issue) articles will help you determine what is selling and at what prices.

Now that you have all that information, let's look at the original questions. Remember the pop quiz? What kind of business are you really in? What goods and services do you provide?

The Product
Asking yourself questions like: What does my product do for my customer? Why? When? Where? How? can lead to conclusions about what business you're in and possibly direct you to new lines or enterprises. Are you the maker of quality frames or selling a decorative wall item that shows the customer's taste, cultural awareness, and status?

The Market
Where is your market, and who will buy? When and why will they buy? Describe your market area, and profile your customer. Owners of $25,000 homes are not as likely to be interested in what custom framing can do for their homes as $100,000–homeowners.

The Competition
Who is your competition? What are the strengths and weaknesses of your competition? Can you get a share of the market? Is there enough market to share? How will your sales strategy be affected by the proximity of your competitors?

The Groundwork
Does it seem like a lot of work? Well, it may be that you'll spend several days finding the information, a few more compiling the facts and figures, and a few more adjusting your business decisions to suit the business climate. Yes, you're right; it does take a great deal of time. Why not just open that store and wait for customers to beat a path to your door for that better–built frame? Why not just sit back and wait for that good old "word of mouth" to bring you customers? Can you afford to wait? A little groundwork can save you a lot of waiting.

2

BOOKKEEPING & ACCOUNTING

First — a general description of what bookkeepers and accountants do. A bookkeeper records those events (expressed in dollars) which affect the financial condition of the business. A bookkeeper or accountant then classifies, sorts, and summarizes these events to give a condensed picture of the financial condition of the business. So many events may affect the business, and so many transactions may take place, that the bookkeeper/accountant must take care to record the course of events and keep the records complete and accurate.

Bookkeeping, then, is the systematic recording, sorting, and summarizing of the events (in dollars) that affect the business financially. Accounting includes and goes beyond bookkeeping. Accounting is also concerned with the analysis and interpretation of financial information and with setting up the bookkeeping system.

Bookkeeping is recording. Accounting is analysis.

Set Up a System

Despite the fact that most frame shops and galleries are small and do not have both bookkeepers and accountants, we still need to record the events and analyze the financial information. You can be the person who records and analyzes the information, or you can hire part–time help or a secretarial service to do the recording. There are also several inexpensive software packages available to use with your computer that will help you set up a bookkeeping system.

However you go about setting up a recording system, it must be done, and you must understand the reasons for doing it as well as the methods.

The Business Entity

First, we need to understand the business entity. In bookkeeping, the business is regarded as an entity that is separate from its owners. This means that the business — not the owners — purchases the supplies and pays the wages. The distinction between the business and its owners is very important in understanding the way bookkeeping records are kept.

A business can do almost anything a person can do; for example, it can borrow money, pay wages, sell merchandise, and rent store space. Remember, it is your business — not you — that pays your wages.

Balancing the Equation

Now we can move on to the basic accounting equation: Assets = Liabilities ± Owner's Equity. Since you have probably heard of it already, let's try to understand it better by breaking it down and defining it.

Assets

Since a business is an entity separate from its owners, it can own property and possess rights. All of a business's possessions and rights which have monetary value are called assets of that business. Cash, land, licenses, inventory, and furniture are all assets.

Liabilities

A business may borrow money from individuals or from other businesses. It may also purchase goods and services with a promise to pay in the near future. This type of purchase is called "on account." When a company borrows money or buys product or services to be billed at a later date, it acquires a debt. The debts are called liabilities of the business.

Owner's Equity

The owner's claim against the assets of a business after liabilities have been deducted is called the owner's equity. It also may be called capital, proprietorship, or net worth. At any time, creditors have claims on the assets of the business entity, and the remainder is claimed by its owner. So, while the total assets of a business may increase or decrease, the change will always cause a corresponding change in liabilities or the owner's equity. The equation A=L±OE will always balance.

The Initial Investment

You're probably wondering what happened to that original investment that you made in the business. It is in there somewhere. The investment is used in the business, and you probably will not take it out until you close down the business. But you can, we hope, make money on your initial investment. After the very first transaction, the owner's equity changes. The owner's equity is not the same amount as your initial investment, nor is it the total of your investments through the life of the business, because the business may have gained or lost assets in the course of operations. The necessary adjustments are made through the owner's equity. From a bookkeeping and accounting standpoint, the equation A=L±OE will always exist.

Business Transactions

Now we can move right on to business transactions. Business transactions are those events, expressed in dollars, that affect the financial condition of a business. Examples include sale of merchandise, payment of a debt, purchase of supplies, or any event recorded by a bookkeeper. Before a bookkeeper will record a transaction, she/he will require some kind of proof that it has in fact taken place — receipts, invoices, daily sales slips, contracts, etc. These business documents are papers we prepare for different transactions. Bookkeeping is a system through which information flows. Disorganized information enters the system in the form of daily business transactions. The system processes this information by recording it, sorting it, and summarizing it. The processed information leaves the system in the form of statements which summarize the events that have affected the business.

INPUT ⇒	THE SYSTEM ⇒	OUTPUT
Daily invoices	Organize	Organized
Receipts	Sort	Information
Payouts	Record	In the form of
Deposits	Summarize	Financial Statements

Financial Statements

The two most important financial statements are the balance sheet and income statement. The balance sheet reports the financial condition of the company in terms of its assets, liabilities, and owner's equity as of a certain date. The income statement reports how the financial condition of the business has changed over a given period of time.

Financial statements are read and used as a basis for making decisions by owners, managers, creditors, investors, bankers, the government, and the public. The information contained in this article is not meant to take the place of your accountant, only to give you a better understanding of the process. If you are fascinated by all this information, go to the local college bookstore and pick up a self–review book or programmed learning aid on the subject or take a course from the continuing education department.

3

FINANCIAL STATEMENTS

Financial statements are typically made up of an Income Statement (which is also called a Profit and Loss Statement) and a Balance Sheet. You may generate these yourself or use a bookkeeping or accounting service to generate them for you. The statements are made at regular periods such as every month, every quarter (3 months), every six months or every year. To maximize your benefit from these powerful financial tools you must understand what you are seeing and how the information for your shop compares to other industry numbers and to your prior years' business.

In order to read anything, it helps to understand the language. Following is a list of terms and information you should know in order to get through this chapter.

Glossary of Accounting Terms

Assets — all the possessions and rights of a business that have monetary value.

Current Assets — those assets which are expected to be consumed or converted to cash in a short period of time, usually a year.

Fixed Assets — those assets which are expected to be consumed or disposed of over a longer period of time than a year. Equipment is an example of a fixed asset.

Liabilities — the debts of a business.

Current Liabilities — debts that are expected to be paid off in a short period of time, usually a year.

Long–Term Liabilities — debts that are to be paid off over a period of time greater than a year. Loans are an example of long–term liabilities.

Owner's Equity — the owner's claim against the assets of the business after liabilities have been deducted. It is also called capital or net worth.

Balance Sheet — a financial statement that reports on the condition of a company in terms of assets, liabilities, and owner's equity.

Income Statement — also called profit and loss statement (P&L), it is a financial statement that reports, in terms of revenues and expenses, the changes in financial condition that have taken place in a business over a specified period of time.

Financial Statements — documents prepared by bookkeepers and accountants which summarize the effects of business transactions.

Inventory — merchandise held for sale in the normal course of business, materials in the process of production, or materials held for use in a manufacturing process.

Accounts Receivable — money owed to the business by someone to whom the business has given goods or services on credit. It is listed under current assets on the balance sheet.

Accounts Payable — money owed by the business to an outside creditor for goods or services it has received. It is listed under current liabilities on the balance sheet.

Notes Payable (long–term liabilities) — loans or notes to be paid by the business over a period of more than one year.

Notes Receivable (assets) — money the company has loaned out, which it expects to be repaid.

Revenue — the amount of assets that a business gains as a result of its operations.

Fundamental Accounting Equation — the total assets of a business, which are equal to the claims by its creditors plus the claims by its owners. The fundamental accounting equation is the basis for every bookkeeping system.

The Income Statement

			Percent Of Sales
	Sales: Art	$85,200	85.2%
	Framing	$14,800	14.8%
	Total Sales	$100,000	100%
less	Cost of Goods Sold	($37,100)	37.1%
equals	Gross Profit	$62,900	62.9%
less	Operating Expenses	($32,600)	32.6%
equals	Net Profit Before Taxes	$36,300	36.3%

The parenthesis indicate that the number inside is subtracted from the number above.

This is a very simplified Income Statement because we have not included the detailed accounts such as salaries, rent, repairs, taxes, advertising, etc., that make up the Operating Expenses.

Cost Of Goods Sold is figured by filling in the following formula:

Cost Of Goods Sold

	Beginning Inventory	$51,000
add	Purchases Plus Freight–In	$29,000
equals	Total Goods Available For Sale	$80,900
subtract	Ending Inventory	($43,800)
equals	Cost of Goods Sold	$37,100

The Balance Sheet

The Balance Sheet is a statement of the Assets and Liabilities of a company at a specific point in time (the end of an accounting period). The Balance Sheet is based on an accounting formula which says that Assets equal Liabilities plus Owners Equity.

ASSETS	=	LIABILITIES	+	OWNER'S EQUITY
Cash		Accounts Payable		Paid–in Capital
Accounts		Notes Payable		Earned Surplus/Defect
Inventory		Notes Payable		
Equipment		– Long–Term		

The Assets must always equal the sum of the Liabilities and Owner's Equity, thus the name Balance Sheet. A typical Balance Sheet looks like:

Assets		National Average As Percentage Of Total Assets
Current Assets		
Cash	$14,700	14.7%
Accounts Receivable	$7,700	7.7%
Inventory	$35,400	35.4%
Total Current Assets	$57,800	57.8%
Property And Equipment		
Framing Equipment	$21,800	21.8%
Other Fixtures	$36,000	36%
Less Accumulated Depreciation	($15,500)	(15.5%)
	$100,000	100%
Liabilities & Equity		
Current Liabilities		
Accounts Payable	$2,500	2.5%
Notes Payable This Year	$700	.7%
Current Long–Term Debt	$12,300	12.3%
Payroll Taxes Withheld	$600	.6%
Other Current Liabilities	$4,500	4.5%
Total Current Liabilities	$20,600	20.6%
Long–Term Debt	$12,200	12.2%
Total Liabilities	$32,800	32.8%
Owner's Equity		
Paid In Capital	$30,000	30%
Earned Excess (Accumulate After Profit Retained In The Business)	$37,200	37.2%
Total Liabilities & Owners Equity	$100,000	100%

As a business owner, we can get two types of information from the Income Statement and Balance Sheet. First, by comparing our performance to that of the national averages, we can fine–tune our business. For example, if the cost of goods sold is 52.3% and the national average is 37.1%, we can assume that we are either not charging enough for our services, or we are not selling enough higher margin merchandise. Likewise, if any of our operating expenses are lower or higher than national averages, we can make changes to bring specific items in linc. Comparisons to the national averages give us a basis for evaluating the performance of our store.

OPERATING RATIOS

The second type of information available to us from the financial statement is operating ratios. Operating ratios are frequently used by banks and other lending institutions in evaluating the performance of the business. Three typical ratios that are used by banks are Working Capital, Current Ratio, and Inventory Turn.

Working Capital

Working Capital is the amount of assets in excess (or deficit) of liabilities.

From the Balance Sheet:

Total Assets ÷ Total Liabilities = Working Capital Ratio

From our example Balance Sheet:

$100,000 Total Assets ÷ $67,200 Total Liabilities =
Working Capital of 1.49 to 1.
($1.49 of assets to every $1 in liabilities)

Current Ratio

Current Ratio is the amount of current assets as a percentage of current liabilities.

Current Assets÷Current Liabilities = Current Ratio

From our example Balance Sheet:

$57,800 Current Assets ÷ $20,600 Current Liabilities =
$2.81 in assets for every $1 in liabilities

Inventory Turn

Inventory turn is the number of times each year we sell the equivalent of our standing inventory.

From the Income Statement and Balance Sheet:

Cost of Goods Sold (take this # from the Income Statement)
÷ Total Inventory (take this # from the Balance Sheet)
= Inventory Turn

From our Example Income Statement and Balance Sheet:

$37,100 ÷ $35,400 = 1.05 turns per year

For any of the ratio analysis to have value, they must be compared to the national averages. Frequently this information is available through trade publications, trade associations, accountants, bankers, and consultants.

This article was revised and updated by William P. Parker, MBA, CPF.

4

THE BUDGET:

A GUIDE TO CASH CONTROL

Every business needs a budget! Next to incompetence, lack of cash control is the most common cause of business failure. This is especially true when the business is growing fast. Flourishing sales bring unexpected expenditures for supplies and payrolls. Soon the gap between receivables and payables widens. With foresight (or a budget), you could see that it will take more than 30 days to completely turn over "what you bought into what you sold." So you're going to need more than 30 days to pay for what you bought. Sounds so simple when you put it in plain English. If you had a budget, you could plan expenditures so they would not overtake your receivables.

In order to make a budget, we will need a bit of information about your operation. Dig into your files and find last year's profit and loss (P&L) statement — also called operating income and expense statement. It should be in the same file with your balance sheet, also called a statement of assets and liabilities. Together they represent your financial statement. Now, I realize that most of you don't keep current financial statements, but you must have one for the end of your business year. Even if you don't know how to read it, we need it to prepare this budget. While you're getting the statements, don't forget a pencil and paper. A couple of sheets of journal paper or columnar accounts sheets will come in handy.

Compile Figures

First, we'll need some figures from your P&L. Take the "Sales," "Operating Expenses," and "Purchases" figure and divide each by twelve. This will give you the average monthly figures. If your expenses added to your purchases exceed your sales, you need help — fast! Of course, these are only average figures, but they will give you some insight into your costs.

Next, we need to analyze these figures. Under operating expenses, you will have fixed expenses — those that will not change from year to year — the rent, utilities, payroll, salary, contract advertising, etc. There will be many more expenses that will vary — payroll/hourly, sales and merchant taxes, bank charges, maintenance, etc. In analyzing your expenses, look carefully for areas that may be out of balance — areas to cut back or increase. These will be more visible after you have had a look at your departmentalized sales figures (you don't have any? — you will). Next, look at the sales figure.

Departmentalize Sales

The P&L will only show the gross sales figure. What we really need is a sales breakdown by department, for example, how many pieces of glass, etc. Granted, this is not easy information to come by if you don't have a computer or electronic cash register with keys for several departments, but you do have this information on every work sheet you write. It just needs to be transferred to some type of tally sheet. Yes, it's a lot of work, but your business is worth it. Even if you only record one month's figures on a tally sheet, the information can really be a deciding factor in your future purchases.

Departmentalize Purchases

Next, study the purchases. The P&L will only show your gross purchases. It will not be broken down into departments, which is what we need for our study. Your checkbook will have these purchases all recorded, and the invoices will tell you exactly how much you spent on specified products. What you need is a journal sheet or extended checkbook to record the purchases in each department as the invoice is being paid.

With departmentalized information such as the above, you can see exactly what you are spending for glass versus the amount you are selling in glass. Starting to get complicated? Perhaps, but look at all this neat information you're finding!

Budgeting

Now comes the crystal ball gazing. Setting up a budget for next year will require you to anticipate your sales. How? Use an educated guess based on last year's sales with something added for better advertising methods, increased popularity, inflation, more employees, and better selling. Anticipated sales are a critical factor in preparing the entire budget, because they will determine both the amount of activity and the timing of expenditures. By working backwards from anticipated sales for each month, the money required to meet that level of sales can be determined. Don't forget to allow time between sales and cash collections. After figuring how much money you'll have to spend, you can determine the departments in which the money will be spent.

Although the prior year's results are where we start in preparing the budget, be careful to look over those results for factors that may lead to different results in the year ahead. Take into consideration the fact that the framing business is seasonal. According to several studies within the framing industry, almost 13% of the year's business is done in December, compared with 6.50% in February. With all this information, you'll be able to make projections for the next year.

Using some columnar accounts paper, list the departments with their sales, then record the expenses related to those departments. Make others for the purchases for those departments. A computer will make quick work of this type of information.

The actual budget you make up will simply be an average of what you can afford to spend (purchases) for what you will probably sell (sales) considering what it will cost you to sell (expenses). Using monthly averages will give you a guide to buying your inventory with relation to your sales.

A rule of thumb? Don't buy more than you can use or sell in a three–month period or more than you can pay for in 30 days.

5

Credit Terms from Suppliers

When you start to buy the products you need for your business, either to sell or use in the manufacture of other products, you'll be dealing with companies on a credit basis. To receive credit from a distributor or manufacturer, you will need to give enough information to assure the supplier that you will be able to pay the bill when it is due. If you have no credit references and are new to the bank with which you are dealing, you may find that you have to pay *pro forma* (in advance), or perhaps send half the price of the goods before they will be shipped.

When you receive an invoice for the goods, it will have "terms" on it. This refers to the method of payment the supplier expects in return for the shipment of goods. Here is a guide to the most common terms of sale, including an explanation of datings and discounts.

Datings

The dating of an invoice refers to the length of time before which any specified purchase discount may be taken. It also refers to the time at which payment for the merchandise becomes due.

For example, terms of 2/10, n/30 (pronounced: two, ten, net thirty) mean that a 2% discount may be taken for full payment within a 10–day period, and that full payment is due thirty days from the date of the invoice. These periods of ten days and thirty days make up the dating of the bill. Future datings are used because most retailers need credit for a period that is long enough to allow them to sell at least part of their purchases and convert them into cash. Several kinds of datings are used.

Ordinary Dating

"Net 30 days" is a good example of ordinary dating. If no specific dating is placed on the invoice, n/30 is assumed to be the period covered.

Extra Dating

The seller allows added time before the ordinary dating period begins. So, if the terms are "2/10 60 days extra," the buyer has 60 days before the ordinary dating of 2/10, n/30 begins.

E.O.M. Dating

The ordinary dating period begins at the end of the month.

Advance Dating

In these terms, the supplier sets a date from which the ordinary dating period begins.

Seasonal Dating

This is similar to advance dating, except that the later date is related to the seasons. As an example, if you have a school art supply section in your store, you may choose to order the supplies you will need for shipment in the summer months. Since the supplier wants to get the product out of his warehouse before the big rush in August, he gives you a seasonal dating to entice you to buy early. Your invoice might start on October 1 at 2/10, n/30 — or whatever date and terms you and the supplier have negotiated.

R.O.G. (Receipt of Goods) Dating

This means that the ordinary dating period begins on the date the goods are received. R.O.G. datings are preferred by buyers located some distance from sellers because with 2/10 dating, the bill may be due even before the shipment has been received.

Types of Discounts

Now, a word or two about discounts. A discount is any reduction in the list or quoted price of the merchandise, which the dealer allows the purchaser to take when certain conditions are met. Here are some of the discounts which may be offered.

Quantity Discount

This is a reduction allowed from the price stated on the invoice because of the quantity purchased. Typically it is based on the amount ordered at a given time. There also may be a cumulative discount (also known as a deferred discount, patronage discount, or rebate) that would apply to the total purchases made within a certain period.

Advertising Discounts

These discounts, or allowances as they are sometimes called, are reductions given by manufacturers for various forms of sales and promotional efforts on the retailer's part. The supplier may give a discount on merchandise the retailer buys in order to take part in the promotion, or he may pay for all or part of the retailer's advertising.

Cash In Advance

Also called *pro forma* — a Latin phrase meaning "as a matter of form." It is usually used when there is a new account without a credit history, or an old one with a shady history. Basically, it means "up front," and it also is referred to as C.I.A. (cash in advance). The seller wants the money before shipping products to the buyer; however, the buyer should receive a cash discount for paying ahead of time.

Cash Discounts

Let's not forget other cash discounts, which are reductions in price given by the seller when the buyer pays promptly. For example, some suppliers of equipment offer a cash discount if a check accompanies the order. That can be a substantial savings.

Anticipation

This practice has all but disappeared but there was a time when a retailer could earn an extra discount, referred to as "anticipation," if he or she was able to pay the invoice before the due date. As an example, the retailer might take the cash discount plus 6% interest on the balance of the invoice for the number of days remaining until the end of the discount period. On an invoice for $1,000, with terms of 2/10, n/30, assume payment is made five days before the end of the discount period. The 2% cash discount equals $20, leaving a balance of $980. But this balance is subject to a further reduction of 6% interest for the five days, which equals 82 cents. So, the actual payment the retailer makes is $979.18. This could add up to a considerable amount on a large invoice with 90 or 120 days dating.

Advantages of Discounts

In nearly every case, it is highly advantageous for the buyer to take the discounts available. Here is an illustration of the savings that may be gained:

On terms of 1/10, n/30, the buyer will realize a savings equal to 18% per annum. Here's how to figure it out. Obtaining a 1% reduction by paying 20 days (30 minus 10) before the due date is the equivalent of eighteen 20–day periods for an entire year (360 days divided by 20 equals 18). At 1% for each 20–day period, the annual return is 18 times 1%, or 18%. Other terms, such as 2/10, n/30, can result in an even greater savings, nearly 40% per annum. As you can see, it is important to take advantage of the discounts offered!

Legal Considerations

You may wonder, with all of the terms, discounts, and "deals" that abound, whether we are all being treated equally. There is a law called the Robinson–Patman Act (1936) which states that a vendor selling in interstate trade may not give a lower price to one buyer than to another under the same set of circumstances. The Federal Trade Commission enforces this law. Inquiries can be made at a law library about the exact regulations contained in the act. Trade discounts are not mentioned in the Robinson–Patman Act; however, the FTC and the courts have ruled that as long as various trade discounts are offered equally to all buyers in a specific grouping, they are legal.

Billing

Many firms send monthly statements, showing the month–end balance of the customer's account. The statement lists the invoices for a period of time, with credits noted for payments made. Some businesses may use "cycle billing" to distribute the work of preparing statements at different dates instead of all at month's end. Others do not send statements. Their invoices may read, "no statements sent, pay from this invoice."

Overall, it is good business to understand the terms on your invoices and statements and to handle them properly.

Part II

Management

6

Pricing the Custom Product

Your first customer of the day walks out of your frame shop without leaving an order. She says your quote to frame her needlework is much higher than that of the shop down the street. The second customer is very pleased with the price you give him on framing the photo of his mother–in–law. He claims to have gone to three other frame shops, and yours is the cheapest by 25 percent.

How do you know if you are charging a fair price? How do you make sure you are generating a reasonable profit for yourself?

Framers do not price goods the way general retailers do. Gift stores take product from a shipping box, price it and place it on a shelf. The customer makes her choice and takes it to the cash register. No customizing of the product is required.

By contrast, the framer adds value to moulding, glass, mat board and other items by customizing them. The problem for picture framers is how to charge for this added value — and how to do it in an equitable manner. The framer does not want to overcharge for large frames while undercharging for small ones. The price charged must include all costs and a reasonable profit to keep the business operating.

What's required is a basic formula to determine prices and allow a fair profit. The following formula can be applied to length moulding, chops, glass, mats, fitting — even picture hangers — to give you a standardized system. The formula provides a fair price for the small frame as well as the large frame.

Working out the formula initially may take you some time — yes, it will require researching your costs of doing business — but with it, you will arrive at a pricing formula you can trust and defend.

The Basic Formula

The *basic pricing formula* is:

ACTUAL COST multiplied by a MARKUP, plus LABOR, equals the SELLING PRICE. Let's define these terms.

ACTUAL COST is the cost of the item from the vendor *plus* any other costs associated with getting that item to your shop and having it available for sales. These additional costs may include:

Freight to your shop

This might mean UPS or trucking charges. If you pick up the item from the distributor, you should still apply the relevant costs.

Waste or shrinkage

Into this category fall the mistakes and scraps of material that cannot be used. Shrinkage includes the goods misappropriated by employees or shoplifted. The number is expressed as a percentage and will vary according to the item. Chop moulding does not generate waste (in theory), while length moulding may generate 15 to 30 percent waste, depending on the quality of the product.

Carrying cost

This is what it costs you to actually have an item in inventory. For chop moulding and other items ordered as needed, this figure will be zero. For in–stock items, this is your cost of money multiplied by the average length of time the item remains in stock. Your cost of money is the interest rate you are paying for your business loans. If you don't have any outstanding loans, then it is the return you could earn by investing your money in a bank, stocks or money funds — if it wasn't tied up in inventory.

Say your inventory turns over four times per year, which means you carry each item in a stock for an average of three months. If money costs 12 percent per year, it costs 1 percent per month. So your cost to carry inventory is 3 percent (1 percent per month times three months).

MARKUP is the standard multiplier you use for items that you resell in your shop (ready–mades, gifts and so on). This number is expressed as a multiplier. In frame shops, it is commonly 2 to 2.5 times.
LABOR is the time and people power required to produce an item. When computing this figure, use your *shop rate*, not the hourly rate you pay employees. Your shop labor rate includes the employees' hourly rate plus the costs of their benefits (unemployment insurance, workers compensation, holidays, vacations, health and life insurance, sick days, etc.) and employment taxes (FICA). The shop rate also includes overhead, which is the cost of the rent, light, heat, business insurance and so on. This is why car repair shops charge $65 per hour for a $12–an–hour mechanic to work on your car.

A quick way to **calculate the shop labor rate** is to look at the operating expenses listed on your 12–month financial statement. Divide this amount by the total direct *labor hours* for the same period. Direct labor is the labor attributed to production in the shop. If your operating expenses are $100,000 a year and your direct labor for the period totals 5,000 hours, then your labor cost would be $20.00 per hour. Your labor cost has to be marked up just like any other commodity that you are selling. The usual markup is two times, so your shop labor rate in this example would be $40.00 per hour.

Pricing Moulding

Let's plug in some figures and apply this formula to pricing length moulding. We want to get a final price expressed in dollars per foot. Once you have worked out the variables in this formula, you can use it to set up a price chart for mouldings. The chart will enable you to price a frame job quickly.

Actual Cost multiplied by Markup, plus Labor, equals the Selling Price per ft.

To figure the actual cost, let's use percentages. The numbers are examples only, and you should use your own figures.

Step One: figure actual cost of one foot of moulding.

Cost	+	Freight	+	Waste	+	Carrying Costs	=	Actual Cost
100%	+	8%	+	20%	+	3%	=	131%

- To figure *freight*, use your own invoices and freight bills to come up with an average cost of freight compared to the charges on the invoice. Don't forget C.O.D. charges.
- The actual *waste* factor on each moulding will vary with the quality. Figure an average that you can use on all mouldings you carry.
- The *carrying cost*, as we have seen, will depend on your inventory turn over and the cost of your money.

Once you've come up with your *actual cost*, multiply it by the standard markup you use to set prices for ready–mades and other items for which there is no labor involved. If your markup is 2.5, and your *actual cost* is 131 percent, your adjusted markup will be 327.5 percent.

Step Two: figure the adjusted markup

Actual cost	x	markup	=	adjusted markup
131%	x	2.5	=	327.5% or 3.275 times

Thus 3.275 becomes the markup figure *to use in the pricing formula for manufactured goods.*

Labor

To figure your labor charge, first determine what it costs in time to build a frame. Included will be the time required to find the moulding, cut it, check the size, replace the scraps, join the frame and touch up the corners. The time will vary slightly for small frames and large ones. The figure we want to use here is the average. For our example, we're assuming it takes 15 minutes (or 1/4 of an hour) to cut and join a frame.

The labor charge per frame is derived by multiplying this figure by your shop's hourly rate. We already found that figure ($40 per hour) by dividing operating expenses by the number of hours the shop is open annually.

The cost of the moulding is expressed in feet, so the labor cost must be converted into dollars per foot. This is done by dividing the labor per frame by the average footage per frame. You will need to check invoices for the past year to come up with your average footage per frame. For our example, we're using 5.5 feet as an average footage per frame.

Labor charge per frame *x* time	*divided by*	avg. frame	=	labor charge per ft.
($40 x 1/4 hr = $10)	*divided by*	5.5	=	$1.82

This has given us a *labor charge per foot* that can be added to the marked–up cost of the moulding. To determine the retail selling price of a moulding with an invoice cost of 50 cents per foot, you'd multiply by the adjusted markup of 3.275 then add the labor charge of $1.82.

Mldg price	x	adjusted markup	+	labor per ft.	=	selling price per ft.
50¢ per ft.	x	3.275	+	$1.82	=	selling price per ft.
$1.64			+	$1.82	=	$3.46/ ft.

The formula works the same way for chop mouldings, although you will need to calculate new figures because there will be no waste or carrying charges, so your *actual cost* figure will be lower. The labor figure will also be affected because you won't need to add in the cost of cutting the moulding.

Mat Board

The pricing formula also works with mat board and other products. Again, you will have to do some research to find the proper figures.

Using the formula, you can make a pricing chart for mat board by determining what portion of a full sheet of mat board you will need for specific sizes of mats, such as 8x10 or 11x14. For convenience, we will use united inches (UI = the length + the width) to determine the size brackets.

Step one is to determine these size brackets.

Sizes	8x10	11x14	16x20	20x24	24x30
United Inches	18	25	36	44	54

Step two is to figure the percentage of a full sheet needed for each united inches bracket. To do this:
divide the united inches figure in half and square it (UI/2 x UI/2).
OR multiply the length 8 by the width 10 = 80.

This gives you the maximum area for the united inches figure. Divide this figure by the area of a full sheet; this will tell you what percentage of the full sheet you will be using.

For instance, if you're working with an 8x10 mat, you have a united inches figure of 18. If you divide that in half and square it, you get a total area of 81 inches. A 32x40 board contains 1,280 square inches. If you divide 81 by 1,280, you get .0633, which means the 8x10 mat is 6.33 percent of a full sheet of mat board.

The % of a 32x40 mat board used when cutting these standard sizes:

United Inches	18	25	36	44	54
Area	81	156.25	324	484	729
Percent	6.33	12.21	25.31	37.81	56.95

Step three is to figure the *actual cost* of a sheet of mat board using the formula we have used above. These are fictitious numbers; you should figure your own.

Cost	+	Freight	+	Waste	+	Carrying Cost	=	Actual Cost
100%	+	12%	+	20%	+	2%	=	134%
$2.75	+	33¢	+	55¢	+	5.5¢	=	$3.685

This means if mat board is sold to you for $2.75, and you add freight, waste and carrying costs, it actually costs you $3.69.

The actual cost, expressed as a percentage, is then multiplied by your markup to obtain the *adjusted* markup. In this case, the formula is 134% x 2.5 = 335% or 3.35.

Step Four is to calculate the selling price of a full sheet of blank mat board.

Cost	x	adjusted markup	=	selling price of a sheet of board
$2.75	x	3.35	=	$9.21

Step Five is to figure the actual selling price for each size bracket on our chart. You'll multiply the $9.21 cost by the percentages determined in Step Two plus a labor charge. Labor is based on the time it takes to find and pull the mat board, cut the mat blank to size, cut the mat, and mark and return the scraps to stock. As an example, we have used a $6 labor fee per mat.

Let's do a calculation for a 20x24 mat board. It has a total area of 44 united inches, which is 37.81 percent of a full sheet of mat board. So the formula is:

Percentage x full sheet cost	+	labor =	selling price for 20" x 24" board
.3781 x $9.21	+	$6 =	selling price
$3.48	+	$6 =	$9.48

Here are a sampling of prices determined with this formula. Prices for the Rag Mat are based on an *actual cost of $19.40* per 32x40 mat board, plus the $6 labor fee.

UI	18	25	36	44	54
Reg Mat	$6.58	7.12	8.33	9.48	11.25
Rag Mat	$7.23	8.37	10.91	13.34	17.05

Glass and Other Products

Glass is priced by the size of the sheet from which it is cut. If your shop has the space, it is advantageous to inventory the sizes used most often. Scrap glass is difficult to store and use, and it is also dangerous. The pricing formula is applied as it is for other items:

Cost + Freight + Waste + Carrying Costs = Actual Cost

Then:

Actual Cost x Markup + Labor = Selling Price

The labor figure for glass will include pulling the glass from stock, inspecting, cutting, returning scrap to stock, and cleaning. Now may be a good time to determine if you should use powder–packed or pre–cleaned paper–packed glass. Because the paper–packed glass is already clean, it saves labor.

The basic pricing formula may be used to price everything in your shop. Not all components of the formula will be used for every item; for instance, some items may not have waste or carrying charges. You must always be careful to include all applicable labor charges in the formula, including labor spent on preparation and cleanup.

Using this formula will keep your shop prices consistent and equitable, regardless of the size or value of the item you're selling, and you will be receiving a fair return on every framing sale.

This article was co–authored by Robert J. Mayfield, BBA, CPF.

7

Customer Service

You are a customer. Each day you go to gas stations, supermarkets, drug stores, convenience stores and clothing stores to be sold a product or service. The level of service and what you expect from the salesclerk change at each of these businesses. We have learned to accept certain levels of courtesy and assistance depending on the type of business. Perhaps you have been waited on by a salesclerk who never actually *looked* at you. In the clothing store, you have had to interrupt an employee from her personal phone call. Amazingly she managed to keep the phone on her shoulder, maintaining her conversation while taking your money. The sales staff at the drug store chat among themselves and, after rattling your keys several times, someone breaks from the group to wait on you while keeping his or her conversation going. Of course, we all look forward to a trip to the automobile license bureau. Be glad it's only once a year.

You are probably saying "*My* people wouldn't do that." Really? Unless they have been trained to your level of courtesy, they may not see anything wrong with that type of treatment. Remember, this generation is not from the "seen–and–not–heard" school of manners. SOME (please note the emphasis) employees are so caught up with the importance of their job they have forgotten the purpose of the job — to take care of customers.

Regardless of the size or scope of your operation, your business is directly affected by the treatment your customers receive. While it may seem obvious that the staff be courteous and have genuine concern for the customer, you must realize that many people in their twenties and thirties have *not* been *waited on*. They shop in self–serve record shops, shoe stores and clothing stores. The only contact with salespersons is to be frisked by them after leaving the fitting room. Your staff should be trained to serve the customer with a positive, non–argumentative attitude while showing courtesy and respect to the customer. Just what constitutes courtesy and respect? It is up to the owner to discuss the appropriate attitude toward the customer and to establish shop policies to handle problems.

Customer Courtesy

Train the employees to treat the customer with care.

- The customer takes priority over everything else.
- The best parking spaces are for the customers — not the employee of the month or the boss.
- A cheerful disposition is the correct one — no whining or complaining. Remarks about being overworked and having an overwhelming personal life are better left unsaid.
- Bookkeeping and housekeeping tasks are not to be done while the customer is in the shop.
- Never begin vacuuming or ringing out the register when a customer is present. That shows disregard and a lack of respect. You may as well tell him or her to leave.
- If you are pricing art when the customer comes in — stop immediately.
- The customer always has the right–of–way in the shop. Open doors, step aside, walk behind and always excuse yourself.
- Never should a conversation take place that does not include the customer. The customer is a guest in your shop. A personal conversation between employees is out of the question!
- Problems should be handled in a whisper or in the back room.
- When an item is not ready when promised, make every effort to reach the customer before it is due. You really lose points if the customer shows up before you have contacted her.
- Hours of the shop are set for the convenience of the customer. Be at the shop at least 15 minutes before scheduled opening so that the shop and employees are ready to serve the customer. Should a customer appear at the door early, he or she should be asked inside.
- A customer is greeted after he or she has entered. Do not pounce. Wait 10 seconds before saying good morning. Give the customer a chance to get in and establish him or herself.

- If you are busy with a customer when others enter the shop — simply acknowledge them with a *Hello* — they are less likely to leave.
- First impressions are important. The entry doors and floor must be clean. The work surfaces and mat and moulding samples must be kept free from fingerprints and nicks.
- Don't ever mock the customer or do anything which creates a "us–against–them" attitude.
- Projects and customer's work should not be left out in front of the shop.
- Music and clothing of the employees should suit the image the store wants to promote. Great care should be exercised when selecting music. Rock and classical music can be equally distracting. Music should not be too loud or even noticeable. Music is not for entertainment. It is used to create a mood and to fill the air when there are more employees than customers.
- Alternative methods of payment, such as deposits, charge cards and layaway plans, are posted discreetly.
- Avoid posting signs in the shop which may "yell" or "demand." The signage should not imply a lack of trust. Signs which state ITEMS LEFT AT YOUR OWN RISK, NOT RESPONSIBLE FOR GOODS LEFT AFTER 30 DAYS diminish customer confidence.
- Never keep a customer waiting. It shows a lack of regard for the customer's time.

Indifference, rudeness, sloppiness, impatience, aggression, and incompetence must be stopped before they affect your business.

The Phone Call

"How much is framing?" "Do you carry pictures?" Questions by phone can try the patience of any employee, but they must be handled properly. The answers may be complicated but each call is an opportunity to show the utmost courtesy and expertise to a client. A phone call may be the first contact a potential customer has ever had with your shop. An abrupt reply will cancel any business this person may have brought to your shop. These questions are asked often enough and they are very important — so prepare the answers. Type them on 4x6 cards and place them by the phones. Most shops will get at least one phone call per day and five or six on Saturdays!

If the person handling the phone call breathes a deep sigh before answering a *stupid question* or has that "annoyed" tone to her voice, you can kiss that customer goodbye!

Develop Policies

Problems in the gallery and frame shop can be listed and the appropriate response planned so that the company has a consistent policy. Develop a booklet of policies for employees to refer to when these situations arise.

Include in the booklet the method in which the shop wishes each situation to be handled, such as:

- Are customer complaints recorded? Are staff members sympathetic towards the customer? Or do they think the customer is lucky to have been waited on in the first place?
- How do you handle angry customers?
- What is the procedure for handling phone calls while waiting on a customer in the shop?
- If a customer says that the mat color is not the one she or he picked out, will the employee defend the honor of the shop and argue with the customer?
- What if the customer changes his or her mind after you have commissioned the work, made the frame, ordered the poster, etc?
- What if the customer wants to return a piece after six months?
- What if a designer orders the piece, pays for it, then her customer hates it?
- What should you do with a piece that has not been picked up by the owner?

These problems happen to every shop. Find solutions that you can live with and write them down. Employees should understand how situations should be handled.

Underselling

Does the staff understand the customer level of expectation? When a customer asks for the least expensive framing, or a *just* a poster — the staff should understand that it is only a defensive comment. The customer has no idea how much the framing or artwork costs. The first–time customer is going to take more time to sell than a *regular* customer. This is an opportunity to educate the customer — help her or him appreciate the framing process or how artwork is developed by the artist. Show the customer all the wonderful things that can be done and several price levels.

In this manner the customer can see that the piece could be framed for $35.00 but it sure looks great at $350.00. Let the customer make the choice of how much it is worth.

Can the staff justify the prices necessary in custom framing? If they do not see the value in custom framing they will downgrade the sale and may not sell the customer what she or he may really want. *Cheap* and *expensive* are relative values that change with each day and product. Your customer may be shortchanged because the salesperson only showed her what she herself can afford.

Don't forget follow–up phone calls to check on the customers satisfaction with their purchase and phone calls when new items come in that may be of interest to that customer.

Customers choose to patronize your shop for a variety of reasons including location and reputation. They will become loyal, repeat customers if the staff is courteous, personable, efficient, helpful, and knowledgeable.

8

Time Management

"Time? What time? Who's got any time to manage? I'm too busy keeping this shop running — supervising employees, checking on supplies, following up on orders, waiting on my favorite customers, putting in displays, paying bills, and seeing salespeople. Give me a break — there's not enough time left to manage!"

Does that sound familiar? If you've ever hired just one person, even part–time, and find you are still vacuuming the floor, you need to get your priorities in order and manage your time better. I realize that time management sounds very sophisticated — something for the corporate big boys — but the same principles can be applied to small shops with two workers. Let's examine a few ways to lower your aggravation level.

First, understand how you are currently spending your time. Second, decide what jobs you must do and what jobs should be assigned to others. Third, establish priorities and focus on improving the quality of time you invest, rather than the quantity. I know you're thinking that you don't have time to figure this out, but you do. If you take a couple of minutes now, you will save yourself a lot of aggravation later.

Tracking Your Time

How is your time spent? Carry a notebook for at least one day (three days would be better), and note everything you do. That includes talking to staff, having coffee, walking to the bank, talking to kids on the phone, balancing the checkbook, writing checks, handling problems in the back room, calling in orders, reading trade magazines, going through the mail, cleaning displays, vacuuming the carpet, even thinking. At the end of the first day, you will have a good idea of what you do during the day.

Then decide how many hours are available for work. Establish a working schedule or calculate how many hours a week you want to commit (a strong word) to your business.

How many different types of jobs are there? List everything and note how much time each one requires. In addition, list the tasks for which you don't have time now but that you would like to work into the schedule.

Now, which tasks are most important? Set your priorities. Make a realistic assessment of all the tasks you've listed, the amount of time each requires and the time you have available. Looks like a budget, doesn't it? You may notice that certain tasks take more time than necessary and that by reorganizing supplies or coming up with a better filing system you can improve efficiency. Perhaps you need a less complicated method of processing frame orders, a faster way to join frames or a way to shorten phone calls.

Delegating Work

Once you've isolated the important jobs, decide who should do the work. Delegate responsibility, or in the case of a partnership, divide up the jobs. This is the most difficult part — giving up all those crazy jobs. When we start our businesses we are often alone and we do everything. As we grow and hire people, we still want to do things our way. I'm not saying that you shouldn't do things your way even once you grow — I'm just suggesting you have someone *else* do it your way. Take full advantage of your employees — they need to be needed. People are much happier on the job if they feel they are important to the company.

Some major areas in a frame shop and gallery that require constant monitoring are: displays, ordering, shows, mailing lists, windows, frames from scraps, names and price tags on display pieces, updating the sample wall, calling customers, and many others unique to your operation. Realistically, you cannot do everything. Once you have set your priorities, the rest should be delegated to your staff.

Training

Your employees should be trained to do jobs the way you want them done and then expected to complete those jobs in that manner. They need information and responsibility and, as your business grows, they should be able to handle much of the work. If you think they can't, you've hired the wrong people.

Organize Your Day

Now that you have your list of priorities in order, organize your day so you can get the most done. Each day write down what needs to be done in order of importance. List only what is realistic for the day — if you put too many things on the list, you'll be overwhelmed and get nothing done. Although you may not be a habitual list maker, organization is the key to controlling your time. It's also fun to cross items off the list! If you plan ahead, you reduce the time you waste walking around deciding what to do next.

Of course, it may take you a couple of days to plan out your time schedule. But spending a few days now will keep you from working past closing every night after your employees have gone home.

9

PLANNING FOR GROWTH

Watching your business grow is a rewarding experience. In the back of your mind from the beginning is some idea of what you want the business to be when it grows up — MY STORE — running smoothly, organized, and profitable. You've pictured it many times: an old Victorian house, busy with gracious, patient, rich customers . . . or was it a grand, black–glass building with a huge but subtle sculpture out front . . . or that chain of mall stores? Whatever the idea is, it will take some skilled planning to pull it off.

At first growth was easy — the business just seemed to grow and grow, and you got busier and busier. Then the pace slowed — there were increases, but not at the pace you had become accustomed to. It's time for a decision. Where do you go next? What do you want to be when you grow up? You have a nice — not huge, but nice — framing business. Do you want to be huge? Do you want more stores? More inventory? More employees? More profit?

There are three different approaches you can take to increase sales: a new or additional location that will bring you into a new market; new products that you have not previously offered to your present market; and new business strategies that you can use in your present location and with your present product line. Let's explore these possibilities.

New Locations, New Markets

Are you looking for a new location or thinking of adding one? A new market area can bring new customers and increased sales, but there are some things to consider. Moving your store even five miles away can change it greatly. Your old customers may not come with you. We all like to think that people will travel thousands of miles to shop at our store; however, marketing studies have shown that most shopping is done within a four-mile radius of a residence — change that to four blocks in New York City and 40 miles in Utah. If you move, be prepared to lose some customers.

When looking for a new location (either for a move or for an additional store), look for a growth area — one where your business can grow, one with new homes and shopping centers — an area that will need you and your services.

Are you considering an area where there is already a shop like yours? Be careful. There may not be enough market to share, and you both could fail.

New Products, Same Location

Adding a new product line should add sales to your shop. Your existing clientele will be the main customers, but new lines also can bring in new customers. The new line should be related somewhat to the goods and services you already offer. Framers, for example, could add artwork, sculpture, gifts or decorative accessories.

You also could become a specialist in a particular service such as gold leafing or restoration of artwork, attracting customers who might not otherwise come to your shop.

Whatever you add, remember that if you want to make significant increases in your sales volume, you must also be prepared to invest sizable amounts in increased inventory, equipment, personnel and advertising.

For example, if you decide to add an art inventory to your frame shop and reasonably believe you can sell $100,000 worth of art per year, an investment in basic art inventory is needed. To realize $100,000 in sales, you will need to sell at least $50,000 worth of inventory (assuming a 50% margin). If you buy only $50,000 worth of inventory, you will have to sell out your complete stock, closing out your brand-new department and giving your customers nothing to look at — as well as giving customers little choice for that last bit of inventory.

If you want your new department to be viable, visible, and successful, you must have stock on hand to sell. The first year, you will probably spend at least $70,000 on inventory, $20,000 for a base inventory and planning to sell $50,000 worth of it to realize your goal of $100,000 in art sales.

Your profit on the first year's sales, before expenses, will be $30,000, not $50,000. (Retail sales of $100,000 — stock investment of $70,000 = $30,000 profit.)

If you project the same sales figures for the second year and maintain the same inventory levels, your profits will be higher. You will need to spend only $50,000 to replenish your inventory.

When you again make your goal of $100,000 in retail sales, your profit for the second year will be $50,000. ($100,000 in retail sales – $50,000 spent for new stock = $50,000 profit.) And you will still have $20,000 worth of stock to begin your third year. But unless you increase your inventory level now — and your sales goals — your profits will remain constant.

Again, these profit levels do not include additional expenses (advertising, additional personnel, equipment, etc.) that you might have to spend to bring in the additional customers. With any new venture into expansion and growth, it will cost money to make money. The profits will be there but not immediately, and only if you plan well to meet the additional expenses.

Same Products and Location, New Strategy

In this plan you keep the same shop and make no major expansions of your product line, but you create a new revised edition of your shop. First, clean it up, perhaps do a little redecorating. A fresh coat of paint will do wonders.

Then plan ways to operate your business at top efficiency. Analyze each part of your business and get rid of waste. Make the most of your own time, your inventory, your employees, your space and most of all, your advertising.

Seek out your customers and sell them what they want. You may currently offer products and services that could bring in more money, but your customers aren't aware of them. Promote what you do. Make samples of unique framing and invite your customers to see them. Get out in public and promote your company.

Making Your Move
The most important consideration of growth and expansion is the cost. Costs can include not only increased inventory, equipment, displays, redecorating, personnel, advertising and promotions, but also the cost of your own time. You will have to decide how much of the planned move you can afford to do yourself — even though you may well have the skill and ability to do it all yourself — and how much you will pay others to do. How much is your time worth to your company? If you are going to be hanging new wallpaper, who is going to run the business?

Any of these plans will take time and money. There are serious costs involved in growth and expansion, and the added profits may not show up for a while. Can you do it? Sure you can, but plan it carefully. Before you make any moves, do some homework.

Stabilize Your Present Business Take a serious look at how your shop is operating and how you got to this position with your business *before* making big changes.

Clarify Your Present Market Your market is comprised of your location and your customer. Your market determines your product. Your customer will buy what he or she likes and leave you with the rest. If you're smart, you will buy more of the products your customers like so you can continue to sell to them. If you buy only what you like, you may begin to accumulate a lot of dead inventory.

The customers you have are a result of your location. Each location has a certain "draw." The draw will determine your customer type — middle–class, wealthy, yuppie, tourist, etc. Most of your customers will come from within a four–mile radius of your shop — the kind of people who are in the neighborhood are the kind of people who are most likely to shop in your store. Sure, we all have customers who come from another town, but they are not your bread–and–butter customers. You may be the best framer in the nation, but you had better be convenient!

Your dollar volume also is related to the number of people in your market: the population that is able to shop in your store. If your immediate market area has 5,000 people in it, for example, and your goal is $500,000 in gross sales, you are expecting each and every resident to spend $100 in your store. Is that reasonable or possible? Fewer customers must spend more than $100 each to make up the difference. You may also have to share your market with another framer or gallery, and that will limit your market share. Study your market closely and try to be realistic in your expectations for your business — your market base has everything to do with your success.

Streamline Your Operations Before you can even think of getting bigger, you must have a firm grip on your present operation. You will need to find the most effective way to handle everything: orders, inventory, deliveries, personnel, the workshop and the office work.

While you are working on the expansion, will this shop be able to run without you? You may also need to refine your business skills. You can do so by picking up a few courses on finance and management at the continuing education departments of your local college.

Streamline Your Inventory All goods must sell. Dead stock is dead money. Dead money is a dead business and dead business is . . . gruesome, isn't it? In the framing business we have a tendency to "stock up." We can't pass up a good price; besides, it will appreciate in value, won't it? Don't give me that "appreciate in value" stuff — did you open a gallery or a museum?

In the retail business you must sell your goods often. A suggested turnover rate for retail goods is three to four turns per year. That means if you carry inventory worth $20,000 net ($40,000 retail), your gross retail sales should be $120,000 for the year. You should have sold (turned over) your entire inventory three times.

Recently a woman who specializes in antique art said that my advice on moving inventory did not apply to her because her stuff just gets older and, therefore, more valuable. When you purchase inventory to sell in the future — 20,000 feet of moulding or a potential antique — it is called an investment and like any investment it has "carrying charges" because you will not get a return on the investment for some time. When the item finally sells the price must have a considerable margin in it to cover the costs involved.

Retailing means selling your goods for a profit and doing it often enough to make a living. If you buy a painting and it does not sell in six months, the fact is it will probably be with you until you *find* a customer for it. Be careful of stock build-up — it can be a fatal mistake in business. Waiting for a type of art or framing to come back in style may take more time than you have to spare. Remember the red, white, and blue mouldings, circa 1976? Streamline your products. Look at your inventory — stock only mouldings that are proven sellers for you. Leave the trendy or unique stuff with the distributors by using chop service. Chop service is a great way to reduce your moulding inventory.

Stock only the artwork you can sell — the key words here are CAN SELL. Make sure you can develop a market for the various kinds of art you choose to stock.

Streamline Personnel Are you using your employees to their full capacity? That doesn't mean having them run around trying to find Mrs. Smith's needlepoint. Give them responsibilities to keep them happy and interested and to keep the store running smoothly. Each job in a shop can be assigned to someone. If you do not have capable people to do the work, get some. You do not have room for ineffective people.

Assign specific tasks to each of your employees and make them responsible for getting the jobs done. If you think you are the only one who can do anything, you *will be* the only one doing it.

Streamline Order Practices Think about how much time you spend ordering chops, glass, mat board and artwork. Organize it by thinning down the number of companies you do business with to the most efficient and reliable. Assign the ordering tasks to an employee.

Finally, things are running smoothly. Now you can look at growth and expansion possibilities realistically and determine which would be the best approach for you and what you want your business to do for you.

10

Economic Survival

On COD with your suppliers?
Put your payroll on Visa?
Is the rent overdue?
Filed your taxes without sending a check?

It's March and you are still paying off your December buying spree. The holiday season didn't save you. Your cash flow is nonexistent. Taxes are due. How could you *possibly* owe taxes? Does any of this sound familiar? If so — get a grip — this situation will not self–correct.

Optimism is the strength of an entrepreneur; however, it will be your demise if you do not face the facts. There is no great sale that will save you — you *must* adjust your business style. Here are several suggestions you may find helpful.

Get Real

To understand your limitations you need to learn what your operating costs are. The *facts* are in your financial statements. If your statements are not handy, simply add several months worth of checks to find out how much you are spending and on what. Divide your expenses (overhead & wages) by the number of days you are open. This figure is what you need to operate each day. It is *not* your break–even point. Breaking even requires the cost of goods to be added to the expenses. If you are a gallery with expenses of $600 per day, you would need sales of $1,200 to break even. That would be $600 for expenses and $600 for product. While you are adding up these expenses, look at excesses. What areas can you trim?

You need goals. How many sales are required each day to break even? Explain this to your employees. Ask them to meet daily/weekly sales goals.

Employees may not understand how retail works. Explain that the reason markup is necessary is that it pays the expenses and their wages.

Stick to Your Market

Do what you do best. Keep a focus on what your business is intended to offer. What products do your customers associate with your shop? It is easy to get sidetracked into other products thinking they will offer the quick buck. The beautiful rack of cards for only a $900 investment looks as though it will bring in extra money — but how much? You will not see a return on your $900 investment until you sell its entire contents four times. That adds up to 2,880 cards at $2.50 retail.

Gross sales	$ 7,200
Original investment	$ 900
Replacement stock	$ 3,600
Total expense first year	$ 4,500
Gross profit	$ 2,700

The $2,700 does not include overhead or the little paper bags you had custom–printed. The gross profit is approximately $8.75 per day or $52.50 per week. That is the equivalent of selling a $100 piece of art or a $75 frame. You could easily increase your sales of existing products by being a better salesperson, encouraging your employees to increase their individual sales, or by following several other suggestions in this article. Put the $900 towards your payables.

Justify All Expenditures

What purchases **must** you make? Examine your spending habits. Search for waste. When buying supplies for the shop or office think thin. Buy enough to get you through a month or two. I know you get a better price when you buy dozens or hundreds, but at this time it is better to buy less and keep the cash close at hand.

Use Chop Services

Yes, you pay more for the service but you have no investment tied up on speculation. Your customer has ordered this product and you will have the money for it soon. With length moulding you invest money in moulding to stock in the shop and this moulding may wait several months before being sold. It, in fact, may never sell. With chop service your investment is in the corner sample. When you place an order, you know you have a sale. If a customer orders 27 frames from the same moulding **then** you may order it in length. If you do not have a pricing formula, mark up your chops at least three times to cover costs.

Consolidate Orders

Decrease the number of companies you buy from so the shipping and COD fee will be a smaller amount of the cost to buy the product. An order for one $12.50 frame or poster may have shipping charges of $2.40 and a COD charge of $4 or more. These charges will significantly reduce your profitability. It can turn a sale into a donation. Purchasing from a local distributor may reduce shipping costs considerably.

Enlist Employees

Explain to employees the need to reduce expenses. They will want to help. They are more aware of your financial condition than you think. Explain the need to reduce expenses — all utilities, wasted mat boards, incorrect orders, wasted wrappings, nails, and time. Employees will make a stronger effort to contact customers and to increase sales if they know you need them to help.

Reduce Payroll

Oh, I know you hate this one but you must use every possible means to conserve money. Cut hours. Examine the jobs each person is required to do. Can people be more productive? Do you really need everyone to come in early each day? Can she or he work a half day? If you can save a total of 20 hours per week at $5 per hour you could save $100 (not including taxes) per week. The big companies call this "downsizing." It works.

Increase Customers' Purchase

Your customers trust you, like your store, like the things you do. Do they know all you can do? Who will tell them? You can make displays in the store or hand out a flier on several products or services you have. These people may only think of you for art or framing and not know how creative you can be. Make a conscientious effort to get your existing customer to purchase more. Casually talk to them about other services you offer, show them your display wall of ideas. Displays can inform customers of such services as dry mounting, photo collages, object boxes, laminating, shipping, and storage boxes.

Raise Your Prices

Am I crazy? Now? When everyone is so cost conscious? Yes, I know that you agonize over the price of moulding. What if your favorite moulding (you know, the one you sell to everyone because *you* like it) sold for $1 more per foot? The retail at present may be $4 per foot, the typical frame job uses six foot, so the cut and joined frame retails for $24. Raise the price per foot — now it retails for $30. Are you going to lose a customer for $6? How about adding $1 to each fit job? Or 50¢ to each mat? It adds up favorably. Low prices will not do your customer any good if you are not in business.

Efficient Ordering System

Look at the system you use to take in the item to be framed. Is the system bulky? Do you have to record the same information 3 times? Since most ordering systems evolve, they often require unnecessary multiple pieces of paper. Each time a number is rewritten it is more likely to be incorrect, resulting in more costly errors.

Get Money Fast

Reduce turnaround time to one week for regular jobs or two weeks for specialty jobs. Hey, it only takes you one hour to do the job, why make your customer wait three weeks? Eliminate calling the customers when the item is complete. Tell the customer when you write up the order that it will be ready in *one week* and you will *not* be calling her unless there is a question about the order. If you do 40 jobs per week, you are making at least 60 calls to reach the customer — what a waste of employees time and phone service. The faster the customer gets the framed piece the happier she is, you get the money, and the piece does not hang around waiting to be damaged or misplaced. Furthermore, the longer she waits, the more she loses interest — she may never pick up the piece.

Check Your Backlog of Orders

Call the customer, tell her you will be delivering in her area next week — when will be a good time to drop off her piece? Explain that you will take charge cards or a check. Do not forget to tell her how great the framed piece looks!

Inventory Clearance

Clean out the excess. The motto in retailing is 20% of your stock is responsible for 80% of your sales. Take a serious look at your inventory. Both art work and mouldings — what is this stock waiting for? If it hasn't sold in the past 12 months when will it? How long can you afford to wait?

Sell the stock you have. Mark mouldings you have in stock on the side with a little dot. Select those when selling to the customer. Put several on "special." Your designers will be delighted to have something to offer the customer that wants a "deal." Call the mouldings discontinued — you did discontinue them, didn't you?

I know artwork is touchy — all you gallery people are saying, "Well if it's worth $200 in June, why is it half price in January?" Allow me to take the mystery out of this. Artwork is a product just like jewelry, clothing, a car, or a fur coat. It must sell to have value. If you cannot sell an artwork it may be you have misjudged your customer's taste.

Try returning it to the publisher in trade for different stock or trade with another framer or gallery. I'm sure you'll find other dealers have a few of these gems multiplying in the back room. Remember the objective is to *sell* the product — you're a gallery, not a museum. If you have unframed art, get it out of the bins and into a frame. Framed art sells much faster. Do not skimp on the framing. Design mats and frames that are currently in style. A look at several of the home decorating magazines will show you what is fashionable. Use "designer" colors in the framing. Each January issue of *DECOR* features new colors and design trends. Put a selection of small artwork (11x14 and under) in a little bin next to the register. This is excellent for impulse sales and it keeps customers busy while you are hunting in the back room for their order. Some artwork can be put on "special" to make room for new inventory.

Rearrange Stock Often

Move the products around so things appear new. They will not only look new to your customers; your employees will also see them differently. Arrange the walls by artist, color or subject matter. Do it at least once every two weeks.

Re–Negotiate Your Rent

This is more probable than you think. If times are slow and your landlord is concerned about empty space, he/she may be willing to negotiate. Explain your financial circumstances. The longevity of your company depends on lowering expenses. Could he/she accept a payment of (*fill in the blank*) less each month for one year? You could reduce the rent by at least one hundred dollars if not more. The landlord could justify the reduction by comparing the lower return against an empty shop and a legal hassle to collect the remainder of the the rent. If possible, you may consider reducing the amount of space you occupy to reduce the rent.

Set Up a Ready–Made Department

Make an area in your shop for ready–mades. It is always of interest to artists and do–it–yourself–ers. Use four or five standard sizes. Make pre–cut mats that include a backing piece. Offer glass taped to a piece of corrugated or foam board. Make frames from your extra stock. Price everything clearly. You might consider pricing them at the "custom made" price then reducing the price for a "Special Offer." Put the display in one corner of the shop. Put a sign above identifying it and place a sign in the window.

Sell Seldom–Used Machinery

Do you have any equipment or displays gathering dust? What are you saving them for? If you ever redecorate you will want something else and the equipment is just getting older and rusting. You need the cash. Use your local distributor, your PPFA chapter newsletter or tell a couple of salesreps that you want to sell it off. You might also check the *Sources* issue of *Decor* for equipment brokers.

About Those Overdue Suppliers

Call them and explain that you will send small amounts. Yes, they will accept $50 a week. If you are still ordering from them and you are on COD they can add $20 (or more) to each order you place, thereby reducing your debt. Example: you order several chops that total $54 plus $6 for shipping and COD. The supplier will add an additional $20 so your order will cost you $80 instead of $60 and you will have reduced your debt by $20. Hey, it's a start. It is more feasible than coming up with the lump sum you owe. It appeases the supplier, allows you to continue to buy product and reduces your debt.

Keep a Positive Attitude

Customers never want to hear that the retailers they know and trust are not doing well. If asked, "How's business?" simply respond, "Just fine, thanks. How are you doing?" If asked how the economy is affecting business, a good response might be, "Oh, we notice it sometimes. Please, allow me to show you a fantastic print I've been saving for you."

So what are you waiting for? Time and money are wasting — get control! Business is like a car. It won't run itself, except downhill.

PART III

ADVERTISING

11

Advertising

Advertising is a relatively quick, efficient, and powerful method for communicating with the public. Unless you have some other consistent way to keep in touch with your customers, you will find advertising a part of doing business, and you must plan and budget for it.

You may be the best framer or gallery owner in the state and not be able to stay in business because not enough people know of your fine products and services. Advertising makes you known to potential customers; however, advertising is not free and you must weigh the costs and benefits of the different media.

How Much Advertising?

With limited funds to spend on advertising, the choice of the medium and the amount of money you spend must be accurate. Be sure that the medium you choose is reaching your potential customer. You may notice the large department store in your city advertises in the newspaper every night, and also on the inside cover of every theater book, cookbook, and yearbook in town. A big store can afford to advertise like that — you cannot! That's image advertising — it's wonderful, but it can be a stretch on any advertising budget.

You can waste money by advertising too heavily or in the wrong medium. A half–hearted effort is often worthless. The type and frequency of advertising you choose depend on several factors:

Your Location

This more than any other factor determines how much you need to spend on advertising. If you are in a strip shopping center or mall, you benefit from the traffic brought in by the other stores. The best reason for locating in a mall or center is this proximity of important stores and services.

Of course, it is essential that you locate next to stores that attract the customers you need. The right location should be close to the homes or offices of your potential clientele.

The Demand

If you are meeting a demand that already exists, you may not need much advertising —your customers will flock to your shop. If that is not the case, you may need to advertise to create the demand. Advertising should encourage people to come in and buy your products and use your services.

Competition

Advertising becomes more important if you must differentiate your products and services from those of the competition. You know that not all frame shops and galleries are created equal — however, your customer doesn't know this. Advertising is the way to tell the customer what makes you so unique!

Business Cycle

An established shop with a solid reputation needs advertising less than a new firm trying to enter the marketplace (except in a fiercely competitive market). When you advertise, you accept some risk in investing in an uncertain future. You will need advertising most — and it will be a greater expense — when you are first entering the market. This is also when your finances are lowest and returns are merely projected.

Your Budget

There are various theories about the best way to set a budget for advertising. You could be guided by the figures compiled by the Professional Picture Framers Association, which show that the average business in our industry spends 2.8 percent of its annual sales on advertising; or you could spend whatever is left in your overall budget; *or* you could advertise whenever you feel like it and hope it brings in enough money to pay for itself!

Any of these approaches may work for you. But don't forget that each business is a unique combination of location, product and customer. An advertising strategy should stem from your company's goals — it should have a relation to the reasons you're in business in the first place.

When to Advertise

The effectiveness of advertising depends on the people in your target market, the number of them you reach, how frequently you reach them, and the content of your message. These four criteria are interrelated. You may choose to do image advertising. This tells the customer what you do but does not ask her to act on it now, only to remember you when she needs your service or product.

A powerful message advertised in a monthly local or personal newsletter is likely to be more effective than a mediocre ad run in the daily newspaper. Repetition is important, but reaching the most likely customers in your community is more important. Look to advertising media that will be effective for your potential customer.

It is important to measure the results of advertising. Though it is hard to establish a direct correlation between sales and specific advertisements, the impact of advertising on revenue generally becomes clearer over time. If you place an ad asking people to respond (to call or come in) and they don't, one of two things happened. Either they didn't see your ad or they were not interested — so you had the wrong market, wrong message, wrong place, or wrong product.

However you choose to advertise, plan your strategy. Make sure you have the right product and the right message in the right place aimed at the right market.

12

ADVERTISING PLAN

You've opened your shop — where are all the customers? Did you think they would fall in off the street? Beat a path to your door? Didn't they notice all the planning that went into this operation? Good grief! How could they pass up this opportunity? Easy; — they don't know it is available to them.

It is up to you to go out and get those customers. You must convince them of the wonderful opportunity they have to spend money in your store. The way to do this is to advertise — before you open and after you are in business.

Planning Advertising

We have all read our share of well–written articles on advertising authored by MBAs who specialize in communications. These articles are often long on theory and short on practice. A small business just does not run the way Harvard thinks it should. In the world of small business, it's the impulsive play–it–by–ear, hope–for–the–best, I've–been–so–busy–I–passed–the–deadline, and I–lost–the–artwork–on–my–desk style of advertising that is the rule rather than the exception.

Small business owners seldom have any idea of how much they have spent or will spend on advertising. I'd bet most frame shops have no plan or budget for the upcoming year. So, let's whip up a plan right now. This will not be difficult — honestly!

What to Advertise

You have a location, a product, and an idea of who, what, and where your potential customer is — you did do your market research, didn't you? Now, all you have to do is get their attention and get them in the door.

Your outstanding qualities are some reasons for the customer to patronize your shop. You have special qualities as a business that another store, even one very similar to yours, does not have. With a plan for advertising, you can accent your good points. Use that paper and pencil to make a list. Are these some of your good points? Experience, trustworthiness, convenience, location, well–trained staff, specialty framing, easy financing for purchases, handsome framing, handsome framers (oops!), large stock, quick service, convenient hours, pickup and delivery services, parking, etc. You can go on and on. Do it!

Unique Qualities

After you have the list compiled, choose the parts you want to accent that will make you look better than your competition. Things that may be obvious to you are unknown to potential customers. Ever wonder why the front doors of small businesses often state "air–conditioned"? It's not because they wanted you to know their electric bill just doubled or because their salespeople were very cool. It's because it is a customer benefit. The list you made shows customers' benefits — reasons for people to want to shop at your store.

Your basic ad will be informational. Tell the customer what you do best, and present your style. The design of the ad may be difficult. Hire a free–lance artist or a small ad agency. Tell them what you want, and ask for a price up front. Have the ad drawn up in at least three sizes to be used in newspapers and pamphlets. The same ad can be used over and over again unless it's for a one–time promotion. Remember, the main idea is "familiarity breeds trust." The more people see your name, the more they trust it. You may want to include a black and white photo or a line drawing of your storefront or building in the ad for greater recognition.

You can also assemble an ad brochure or folder to outline your strong points. Be sure to mention the types of art that you carry. Don't forget a list of the basics — shop name, complete phone number, and full address, including city and zip code. Shucks, you might say, I can remember all that stuff. Well, even with twenty years of advertising experience, I once placed an ad in a statewide magazine that originally ran in the suburban community in which our store is located. the advertisement had no area or zip codes and used the name of the suburb instead of the metropolitan area. Actually, I never would have noticed it if it hadn't been for a new customer who told us how much trouble she underwent (thankfully!) to locate us.

Advertising Options

Now you know what you want to say. How and where are you going to say it? I'll outline just a few of the many ways to advertise. These are some of the most popular if not the most obvious.

Yellow Pages — Besides the metropolitan phone book, you can advertise in the suburban one and under many different headings. Rates vary according to population reached. The ad is long lasting and right in there with the competition. Study ads in other cities. Try to make yours stand out in the crowd. Do you want yours to look exclusive — or like "frame city"?

Direct Mail — This includes postal delivery or distribution by an independent hand–delivery service. It gets your message through without a lot of competition. Direct mail acts immediately or not at all in most cases. It asks the recipient to take action now. It will be tossed unless it's educational, a catalogue, a coupon, or something to save (a pretty post card?).

You'll need a potential customer list. There are list brokers in most major cities — buy a list. Brokers have every possible combination available by area, sex, income, occupation, type of car driven, etc. I bought a list of single males between the ages of 45 and 60 who drive Ferraris. Granted the list wasn't long, but it was worth every penny.

Other sources of lists are the Chamber of Commerce, the Better Business Bureau, and civic or social organizations. You may have to join, volunteer for something, or make a donation to get the list. What it's worth in terms of your time or money depends on how important you think the names will be. Don't forget the local art groups, especially the patrons of the arts! If you are going for a certain area, you can use a city directory at the library or buy one for your own use. Absolutely everyone you have

ever known should be on your first mailing list; you can weed them out later. In the beginning, you need them all.
Billboards — These are not very common to small business, but they are not as expensive as you may think. Call the company in your area to get a price. You can always say "no." If you do use billboards, be sure to ask for specific placement. Design a strong visual message with wording that is to the point so that it can be read quickly.
Metropolitan Newspapers — Consider the size and cost for a one–shot item. Rates vary widely with circulation. Do you need the coverage of the large paper, or would the smaller community paper be more suitable? Papers are read by the more educated; 81.8% of college grads "read a paper yesterday."
City and Regional Magazines — These publications appeal mostly to upscale trendsetters involved in community life. The magazine has a longer life — generally "hangs around" the house longer — than a newspaper, and is usually reread.
Radio — Listening audience will be profiled by the station. Pick a station which has a programming style with which you want to be identified. Regular radio advertising keeps your name around. Ad salespeople in this medium are usually sharp and persistent.
Promotional Pamphlets — Small ad books for the ballet, art theater, symphony, community art shows, horse shows, ladies club bazaars, and many other events have advertising. These are tough decisions. I look them over carefully. I look at the likely recipient of the booklet — is it my style of customer? Will he or she get a chance to read it? Watch for the circulation promised on these, it is often exaggerated.

How about the use of donations for door prizes, ads for year–books, and sponsoring marathon dancers, runners, and skippers? Yes, these are worthwhile projects, and they need support. They do not come under advertising, unless you have bought the whole campaign — all 650 marathon skippers are wearing your logo on their backs, and there is television coverage. Get the idea?

As you can see, there are many opportunities for you to advertise. Where do you start? How about the dart board method? Use your instincts, select your favorite medium and give it a try. You must advertise, but not all methods work the same for all shops or in every market. Some media will be better for you than others — you'll have to experiment.

Part IV

Commercial Sales

13

CORPORATE SALES

Commercial accounts! Corporate art collections! Investment art! Contract framing! Is this the BIG TIME for framers? It could be — but it will demand attention to a few areas of your business.

Special attention to your selling practices, organization, and pricing policies will determine your ability to make a profit or loss from a corporate job. Many framers are so excited when they get their first corporate account that they don't charge enough to cover all the costs to make the job profitable.

You need to concern yourself with three areas that will be different from the regular in–house sales. You are going to need a salesperson, a sales plan, and a way to keep track of both the person and the sales.

The Salesperson

Someone has to make the calls on these accounts. The right personality for outside sales is difficult to find. The person should have a "feeling" for art and framing, but he or she does not need direct knowledge of the field. A training program with an introduction to the industry would be a great help to the person, and information about the specific products you expect her or him to sell will be necessary. The good salesperson can sell anything!

The ideal salesperson has the right mix of empathy and ego: empathy for the customer's situation, and ego to get the sale. A healthy ego is very important to a salesperson — she or he needs a "yes" from the customer, which comes from getting an order and winning the customer's confidence. The "yes" also yields a feeling of accomplishment for the salesperson.

This is, after all, a rough business — making cold calls; getting turned down; having people slam the proverbial door in one's face. Outside sales is no place for the timid. It also requires a great deal of discipline to maintain the pace required to make a living. The person must be a self–starter and very responsible. Good grief! Don't forget enthusiasm! A salesperson has to be enthusiastic about the goods he or she is selling.

Job Description

A job description for the outside salesperson might include the following points:

- Title
- Manages self, time, territory, accounts
- Responsible: to the owner or manager of the business
- Primary function: to develop and expand the present customer base
- Commission schedule (In addition, you can expect to pay the person a salary for six to eight weeks before going to straight commission)

Evaluation

Results is the name of the game. If your salesperson is not selling, there are reasons. Find out what they are right away. Using an individual sales record will help you determine the strengths and weaknesses of each salesperson. The employee should be responsible for the maintenance of this record on a weekly basis.

Individual Sales Record

Weeks:	1st	2nd	3rd	4th	5th
Contacts w/ Purchasing Agents/CEOs:	___	___	___	___	___
Phone Calls Made:	___	___	___	___	___
Cold Calls Made:	___	___	___	___	___
Survey Appointments Made:	___	___	___	___	___
Survey Completed:	___	___	___	___	___
Proposals Delivered:	___	___	___	___	___
Sales Made:	___	___	___	___	___
Proposals Pending:	___	___	___	___	___
Commission Dollars Earned:	___	___	___	___	___
Referrals Received:	___	___	___	___	___

Note: a survey call is visiting a business, looking around, and estimating the company's need for art/framing.

A structured weekly meeting between you and a new salesperson should be scheduled as soon as the training program ends. The conferences should continue as long as both you and the salesperson feel they are of value, but at least through his or her 12th week. Your objectives in the conference should be the following:

- To assess the prior week's performance
- To assess plans for this week's and next week's prospecting and sales activities
- To intensify the salesperson's desire to meet certain objectives
- To identify training requirements and plan activities to help meet specific needs
- To consider the types of art/framing sold most often. This will give you a clue as to the amount of knowledge your salesperson has. She or he will sell what is most familiar.

You may also want to address the following concerns:

- Where is your salesperson making calls?
- Does he/she get inside the door, past the receptionist to a person with the authority to purchase?
- What is his/her sales pitch?
- How does the salesperson dress?
- How does he or she make the presentation?

Remember, your image is at stake here, too. Don't let problems slide. Maintain control of your outside sales through communication.

The Sales Plan

Now that you've got this great salesperson, you have to help him or her out with a plan. To outline your plan of action, you should consider the following:

- The products or services to be sold
- The presentation of the products
- The sales pitch for the services and products
- The audience to whom the products will be presented
- Back–up information, such as fliers or brochures to leave behind or send ahead
- An advertising campaign or direct mail program
- Extra services you may provide, such as pickup and delivery, payment plans, hanging and maintenance, and leasing and rentals

Keeping Records

Now to the really fun part — bookkeeping! In order to control the information generated by the outside sales program, you are going to need the following:

- An accounts receivable department, complete with invoices, statements, credit applications, credit policies, terms, and discounts.
- Payroll accounting for the sales commissions.
- A journal to record this type of sale separately from your regular cash sales.

Networking

When selling commercial accounts, it pays to be visible. Join the chamber of commerce and any other local business groups. The more people you know, the more likely you are to make sales. You'll always see plenty of real estate agents and insurance sales people at any civic function. Customers feel more comfortable buying from someone they know, even if they only know that person socially.

And here's a final thought. Train your salesperson (and yourself!) to take a good look at the customer as the presentation is being made. Ask who is the decision–maker in the group — you do not want to waste your time and hers by holding a presentation for people who do not have the authority to buy the product. As an extension of that point — the person at the reception desk is seldom in a position to purchase product. When the receptionist says the company doesn't need any artwork and you believe her — you just took a *no* from a person that can't say *yes*.

14

Volume Framing

What an opportunity! The local hospital has asked you to bid on the cost of framing 800 pictures. This is your chance to get your foot in the door with volume framing. You really want this job, and you know the only way to get it is to put in the best bid.

Think hard before you get carried away with enthusiasm. Volume business is not at all like retail. The buying, the space required, the time spent in manufacturing, the method of payment, and possibly the quality of the product are all distinctly different.

There are *five key areas* of volume framing to consider before you can successfully undertake such a project.

1. Figuring Your Costs

The bid you make on a volume framing job will affect the success or failure of the whole project. But how do you go about determining a price? Do you begin with your standard retail prices and give the company a discount? No. A volume job must be figured on its own merit. The formula to follow is *materials plus labor plus profit.* I realize many of you are willing to minimize profit to get your foot in the corporate door, but be very careful you do not underestimate your product, or you will end up paying the difference.

Even if you're willing to accept a percentage of profit that's smaller than usual, make sure the figures in your bid include every component of the frame — down to the wall bumpers — and carefully estimate time and labor costs. If you incorrectly estimate the cost of a volume framing job, the lessons can be very expensive.

2. Organizing the Shop

In addition to bidding correctly, you need to realize that production will be different with a volume job. Let's suppose you own a frame shop that's approximately 1,000 square feet in size. The average shop makes 2,000 frames per year — about seven per day. An order for 800 frames is almost half of your entire yearly production and would normally require five months to fill.

Obviously you have a few adjustments to make in order to get the job done in a much shorter period of time. Do you need to hire more staff? Do you need to go to an assembly production line? Do you job out parts of the order? Do you buy frames that are already chopped and joined? You need to know how you are going to put those 800 frames together before you even make the bid.

Furthermore, are you certain this order can be done on the premises? Do you have enough space and enough equipment to keep the job moving? You may have to use temporary quarters to process the order, resulting in additional costs for rent. If so, those costs also need to be figured into the bill.

3. Choosing Suppliers

When you first started your business, the hardest thing to learn was how to purchase supplies. It is an art in itself to find the right supplier, the perfect product, a fair price and prompt delivery service.

This learning process will begin again, because the suppliers you currently deal with are not necessarily the ones you will use for a volume job. You should look for companies who not only can supply frames, glass and mats pre–cut, but also can guarantee their delivery dates and provide consistent quality.

If you're also buying the art, you should investigate companies that sell reproductions in bulk for very low prices. These companies are pretty low–profile and seldom advertise, but you can talk to sales reps and other framers to get names of some suppliers you can try.

Another thing to keep in mind: Once you order art and framing materials for 800 pieces, you'll need to find storage space for the supplies as well as the finished frames.

4. Making Sure You Get Paid

It's crucial for you to understand how your corporate buyer plans to pay you. Large companies require that you involve them only after you finish the job. If it takes you three months to complete it, you are going to need money up front to buy materials and pay your framers.

Where will you get this production money? Perhaps you have several thousand dollars saved for just such an opportunity. If not, the money will have to come from a bank loan, using the purchase order as a collateral, or from the company you are working with in the form of an advance or deposit.

You may not get full payment instantly even when the job is delivered. Large companies often delay payment for 90 days or more. Having a signed purchase order doesn't really help. What you need is the personal guarantee of someone in charge. Keep in contact with that person. Ask him or her to trace payment and to hurry it along because you need it. Forget your pride; don't be afraid to ask plainly for your money.

One last note about money: Don't assume that the company you're working with is solvent. You can't judge its ability or willingness to pay bills from the looks of the lobby. If you do not belong to a credit reporting agency, ask your banker for an opinion before you accept the job. Explain the job to the banker; he or she will be able to get financial information quickly.

5. Taking Care of Follow–up Problems

The corporate job isn't always finished after it's delivered. If something breaks in shipping or within the first year after you've installed it, the company will expect you to repair it. This doesn't pose a big problem if the corporation is nearby, but suppose you've sold 800 pieces to a company 500 miles away?

I once had to find a framer in Japan to take care of some broken frames for a corporate order I had shipped there. You need to know in advance if you can afford to hire an out–of–town framer to make repairs for you.

Management of a volume framing project can be quite awesome. Be prepared. This could be a great opportunity for you, as well as a great learning experience. Be certain of the price and the delivery time you quote, or you will pay dearly for your education. Getting a foot in the door may prove to be very painful.

15

Leasing Framed Artwork

The economic conditions under which we are doing business have brought us to new and different ways to purchase what we need. We know businesses need framed artwork for their offices, but when budgets get cut, artwork is often the first item to be left out. To offset this, leasing has become an important selling tool. A lease, with an option to buy, means commercial customers can get what they need all at once. They can pay for it over a longer period of time than would be possible with installment payments and may get tax benefits as well. Leasing is most popular during economic times with high interest rates.

Leasing of framed artwork can eliminate bookkeeping and collection problems and encourage larger purchases. Using a leasing company to handle the financial end of the sale can simplify things.

What Is A Lease?

A lease, in this instance, is an agreement between your customer and a leasing company. Under the terms of the agreement, your customer receives framed artwork for a specified period of time and for a specified price. Your customer has the option to purchase the artwork, generally for a minimal amount over the terms of the leasing agreement.

The lease is arranged by you, the retailer. The leasing company, upon acceptance of the lease, pays your gallery the total price of the goods, including any delivery and hanging charges. The benefits are many. The customer gets the goods right away. The purchase is expensed rather than capitalized — meaning that the customer pays a small amount each month that can be claimed as an expense on his or her tax return. And best of all, you receive the full purchase price at the time of the sale.

Nothing changes your responsibility to, or your relationship with, your customer. It's as if the sale were a cash purchase. Leases can be written for anything — artwork, wall hangings, mirrors, and sculpture. These are referred to as "wall decor."

Leasing would be viable for a product(s) priced higher than $2,000. If the product is priced less than $2,000, a simple payment plan would be used.

How Does It Work?

Consider this scenario. You are at the customer's office. A decision has been made on the artwork to be used in the office. You give your customer a price of $5,000 for the job which includes four offices and a lobby. The customer balks, saying he wasn't expecting to put out that much money at one time. Here are your options:

1. You can cut your prices.
2. The customer can choose lesser–quality items.
3. You can do one office at a time.
4. Or you can use a leasing company that will finance the $5,000 for six years for a monthly payment of $114.04 based on 18% interest.

INTEREST AMORTIZATION TABLE*

Amount	1yr.	2yrs.	3yrs.	6yrs
$ 500	$45.84	$24.97	$18.08	$11.41
1,000	91.68	49.93	36.16	22.81
3,000	275.04	149.78	108.46	68.43
5,000	458.40	249.63	180.77	114.04
8,000	733.44	399.40	289.22	182.47

**based on 18% interest rate. Actual rates may vary.*

The leasing company will provide you with a lease agreement and credit application for your customer to fill out. The forms will require the normal information — bank and business references, officer of the company, etc. When the credit is approved, the artwork will be delivered to the customer, and a signed delivery receipt, along with the copy of the invoice, will be presented to the leasing company.

What if the customer doesn't make the payments? It's not your problem. The leasing company will take care of delinquent accounts in its own manner. Should it repossess the goods, the leasing company may contact you to buy them back.

What Are Your Responsibilities?

Your responsibility to your customer as a framer is the same. Suppose the glass breaks. If it's your fault, fix it free of charge. If it's the customer's fault, charge for the service. You may want to offer a maintenance agreement to your customer. If you sell a maintenance agreement, it's between you and your customer and would not be included in the lease. The agreement would be like any you may have purchased on a home appliance or office machine.

Servicing a product can be costly. If glass breakage is the problem, the artwork will have to be picked up and brought to your shop to replace the glass. Then the artwork must be delivered back to the client and re–hung. This can be very costly. Determine your maintenance charge based on the replacement value of the artwork and the travel distance required to repair or replace merchandise.

Leasing to New Businesses

If your customer does not have a credit history, he or she may have to pay a higher rate and/or a larger down payment for a leasing agreement. The leasing company will rely on you to make some sort of judgment of the worthiness of your customer. (If the name of your customer's business is Midnight Movers — don't press your luck!)

Finding a Leasing Company

To find a leasing company, check in the Yellow Pages directory under "Leasing." It's best to look for one that leases office equipment. Call the leasing company, and explain what you are selling. The leasing company will probably have a minimum amount that it will finance. Some companies will pay you a small percentage of the value of the lease for using their leasing company rather than another.

Financing the Lease Yourself

Financing a lease agreement on your own will be complicated. The IRS rulings to cover leasing are many and change often. There are many state and federal laws with which you must comply. You'll need a lawyer and an accountant to draw up the lease agreement. You'll also need a full–scale a full–scale bookkeeping department to maintain and process credit applications, billing, and collections.

If you are going to lease a work of art that *may* increase in value — really increase, say thousands of dollars over a five–year period — then you've got trouble. The IRS is very touchy about items that appreciate in value. You'll need the advice of an accountant, and perhaps need to get a "private letter ruling" from the IRS stating how it will be handled. But leasing for the majority of artwork on the market is not a problem since the piece, just as any piece of furniture in the office, will decrease in value.

Legally, (we are talking the Feds here), leasing can be very tricky. The key areas are sales tax and assets. Who owns it? How much is it worth? Was property tax paid? Was the sales tax paid and at what value? Any payment arrangement which is made and completed within a one year period is of little concern to the IRS; however, once you get into an agreement for 13 months or more, the IRS has rules, regulations, and paperwork which change yearly, of course.

16

CREDIT DEPARTMENT

Business could be so much simpler if all sales were for cash only! There would be no bad debts, fewer returned goods, and much less bookkeeping. The chances are, though, that you will have to give credit in order to get the most out of your business. The accounting term for carrying your customer's charge accounts is *accounts receivable.*

The definition of *accounts receivable* is debt owed to your firm by customers for goods or services sold to them in the ordinary course of business. Whenever your shop makes an ordinary sale to a customer and does not receive cash payment, it grants trade or consumer credit — and creates an account receivable. (Trade credit is granted to other businesses; consumer credit is granted to individuals. Otherwise, both types of credit are essentially the same.)

An Investment in Credit

On your firm's financial statements, accounts receivable are shown on the balance sheet as a current asset. This department is considered an investment because you are financing or loaning money to your customers to enable them to buy goods from your store. With just a few sales on charge accounts, you can build up a considerable investment in accounts receivable.

In the United States, most business sales are credit sales, so most business firms have substantial investments in accounts receivable. If you look at most of your suppliers, you will discover that 90% of their sales are "on account," with the remainder paid by "check with order" or COD.

So then, if you're planning to do business the "American way," you're going to need to set up a credit department.

Credit Terms

Once you have decided to have a credit department, you need to set the terms under which you will extend credit to your customers. Credit terms are a specific set of conditions under which your firm will allow another business or an individual to open an account. The terms have two primary parts: the credit period and the cash discount offered.

Credit Period The credit period is the length of time a firm extends credit on a sale. It is usually stated as a net date. If, for example, a firm expects payment in 30 days from the date of the invoice, the credit terms are net 30.

Notice that the terms are from the date of invoice. That means that you must get the invoice out fast if you expect to receive the money within the terms you have stated.

Credit periods are fairly uniform within the industry, but firms can and do lengthen their credit period to stimulate sales; however, you should realize that longer credit periods will also cause a higher level of receivables.

Cash Discounts Many firms offer cash discounts to induce customers to pay their bills early. (A cash discount is different from a quantity discount, but the latter is a price concession made to large quantity purchasers.)

If a cash discount is offered, the credit terms will reflect the amount of the discount and the discount period, which is the length of time the discount is offered. Customers who forgo the cash discount are expected to pay by the net date.

Specifications

A complete specification of a firm's credit terms has three parts: the amount of discount, the discount period (or date), and the credit period (or date).

For example, the most common credit combination is a 2% discount if the invoice is paid within 10 days; otherwise, the invoice must be paid by the 30th day. The amount of discount is 2%; the discount period is 10 days; and the credit period is 30 days. The terms are written in compact form as "2/10 net 30."

If, instead, there were a 3% discount, a 15–day discount period, and a 60–day credit period, the terms would be written "3/15 net 60." In this example, any customer who paid by the 15th day would receive a 3% discount. If the customer does not pay the bill by the 15th day, then he or she is expected to pay it by the 60th day.

Other Terms

You may, of course, offer other terms, such as *30/60/90.* In this case, you expect one third of the bill to be paid at 30–day intervals. It is up to you to decide what you can afford to support in the way of credit terms; then state your terms in writing, and stick with them.

You also may choose to limit the amount of credit any customer may receive by imposing a *line of credit limit.* This will be necessary unless you have unlimited supplies of funds and capital. As the seller, you limit the dollar amount of accounts receivable allowed to each customer. When the limit is reached, future credit sales are denied until the customer's account is sufficiently reduced to accommodate the new order. (This is the same type of limit used by bank charge cards.)

The alternative to denying a sale to a buyer who has reached the limit is to raise the customer's line of credit and permit the order to be filled. Whether you choose to do this depends on the customer's credit history and whether your firm's credit policies are *tight* or *loose.*

Overall Credit Policy

A firm's credit policy may be defined broadly as being somewhere in the range between tight and loose. Firms with tight credit policies tend to have relatively short credit periods. They sell on credit only to those customers who have the highest credit ratings. Firms with loose credit policies tend to have relatively long credit periods. They sell on credit to a broader range of customers, including those with relatively low credit ratings.

On a "net 30" invoice, a firm with a loose credit policy may not push for payment until 60 or even 90 days. On the other hand, a firm with a tight policy will call a slow–paying customer on the 31st day.

Your credit policy can have a major impact on the firm's sales, costs, and profitability. If other factors are equal, firms with loose credit policies have higher costs.

As with most financial management decisions, your decision to commit funds to accounts receivable involves a tradeoff between your costs and benefits. Your problem is to compare the costs and benefits involved to determine the best level of receivables for your business.

Sales on credit can get out of hand if they are not controlled with firm policies, such as requiring a completed credit application before allowing customers to charge their purchases. After all, you are entitled to certain information about the company or individual — they are borrowing money from you!

If you're going to give credit, use a professional approach. Set up firm policies, put them in writing, and secure adequate information from your customers in order to make wise decisions.

Part V

Questions & Answers

The best of the *Ask The Experts* from 1983 to 1993
by Vivian C. Kistler

General Business

I've been in business for two years, and my business is starting to show a profit. My husband is considering leaving his job to help with my shop. Should I incorporate the business when he joins me in the shop?

A. Incorporating your business is a decision that you and your accountant, and perhaps your attorney, will have to make. Your accountant will tell you the pros and cons of incorporating and alternatives available. The main considerations are taxation and liability.

Your local Small Business Administration (SBA) has many pamphlets that explain the different methods of doing business, including Subchapter S, which may apply to your situation.

I just opened my frame shop in February. There are so many distributors and manufacturers to do business with. How do I choose which ones to deal with?

A. Look for a company that can offer you a good product, quick service, and a sales representative to call on you. Don't overlook the value of the sales representatives in this industry — they are very willing to help you, and they are generally trustworthy. Since they will be calling on you often, they will give you their best, knowing they will have to face you again the next time they are back in town. They want to make you a repeat customer. They also attend trade shows and are good sources for the latest supplies and information.

You will notice that moulding manufacturers and suppliers usually offer a particular type of moulding, such as European imports, fancy period styles, or traditional domestic mouldings. Since companies tend to specialize, you may need to do business with two or three different companies to offer a well-rounded selection to your customers. But if you deal with too many companies, you will probably be placing small orders, making it difficult to meet minimums required to place orders economically. Also, it is generally better to be an important customer to two or three big companies, instead of being an occasional, one–frame customer to several companies.

We have been framing in our home for 14 months and are planning to rent a storefront. My partner and I have come up with several names, but I won't tell you the name of our shop because I've heard you speak at the Learning Center during several Art Buyers Caravan trade shows, and you mention your dislike for "cutesie" names. What is your suggestion for selecting a name?

A. You have certainly struck a nerve! The names I dislike include those that play on words, sayings, movies, clichés and, let's not forget, the unpronounceable. I will testify that some frame shop and gallery owners spend more time conjuring up incredible names than they spend setting up a business plan. Whew! Now that I have that out of my system, I can get to the question of what to name your business.

The names of the giant retailers, the best restaurants, and even the car dealers carry the names of the owners. You just know that somewhere Mr. Neiman and Mr. Marcus are concerned that each customer is satisfied.

The name of the store should relay to the customer some hint of what it sells and where it is located. This makes life easy for the customer — not a guessing game.

As an exercise in naming a business, list your personal name/names, street address, shopping center name, area, city, state, and main product lines. Try combinations of these until you arrive at the right name. Select a name that will help the customer identify you.

How can a framer who has developed (invented) a tool for framing get his idea into production without having the idea pirated? What companies do this type of thing?

A. I sure hope you have invented a "dust magnet" that works through glass! If you have, and you not only have the idea but could describe it precisely in written and pictorial detail, you may be eligible for a patent. Your tool would come under the category of utility inventions of the U.S. Patent Law. A patent will keep others from using, manufacturing or selling your product without your authority; however, it will not keep them from improving on your idea and patenting their own "new" product. Even your rights to exclusivity will expire in 3–1/2 to 17 years.

As you may have guessed, it's an involved process. You might consider selling the plans and rights to manufacture the tool to an existing company. They may already have a market for it.

I consulted a book titled *Legal Handbook for Small Business* by Marc T. Lane and published by MAACOM. You may want to read a bit before consulting a lawyer.

I hear a lot of talk about "networking." How could this help in picture framing?

A. Networking is one of the "buzz" words in the business community and for good reason: it works. You can apply it easily to any type of business, especially picture framing or any similar service business where trust and word of mouth are important.

A network is a system of personal contacts through which friends, professional colleagues and business acquaintances exchange favors and information. The "old boy network," the best known, is well–entrenched in the business community. There are formal and informal networks. Professional associations, community organizations and local service clubs are formal networks for making useful contacts. The more people you know and the more people who know you and what you do for a living, the more successful you will be in the business community. All people prefer to know the person from whom they will buy a service or product. Your local chamber of commerce is an excellent place to start. All the people there are interested in the well–being of the business community. They are ready to welcome you and introduce you to others. You may need to volunteer for some type of community service — but that's how you meet people — and the more people you know, the better off you'll be. Conferences, business luncheons, after–hours socializing and attendance at art–oriented functions can all serve to expand your base of customers.

The business card symbolizes networking. Each card you collect is a potential contact; each card you give out will circulate so that you can be recognized in the community or "network."

Networking serves a variety of useful functions for the small business owner. It can help you: recruit good employees, obtain and exchange information, hire CPAs, get credit recommendations, get leads on local jobs, get personal referrals, and get the scoop on local available property.

Check into your community, and find some groups to join. Certainly, look for groups that you will enjoy working with but that will also help your business.

I will be opening my gallery and frame shop this fall. I saw several computer systems at Frame–O–Rama. Should I put in a computer system now or wait a few years?

A. Now. When you start out, you will have all your information at hand or in your head. Very often it is the owner/founder who does all the selling, buying, frame making, and office work; however, the business will become complicated with employees, more customers, more stock, and more money. You will want to control all of this. Putting in the computer now will be most efficient.

The software packages made for our industry are great. They will help you inventory materials used for framing, maintain a mailing list to keep track of customers, inventory artwork under many headings, track customer purchase records, process frame work orders, store sales history, and schedule work orders. In fact, you can price and write the work order while your customer is at the counter. The system also could act as a sales register.

Each software system has certain procedures you may require. You will have to decide how much you expect a system to do. Check out the companies producing software before buying. How long have they been in business? Has this software actually been in use for at least one year? Can you contact one of the users? You do not want to be a test market.

If you start *without* a computer, you will need work order forms, an electronic cash register, a scheduling book, and a whole batch of 3x5 cards and files to hold them. Not to mention the many forms you will need to control inventory and sales.

You might as well get started on the right foot — get a computer now.

We have been in business for 12 years in the same location. Business is good but has leveled off. We want to keep this store for my partner to run while I open a second store. Any hints?

A. Sure, I'm loaded with hints. In fact, I'm loaded with major suggestions! First, stabilize your present business. It must be running smoothly before you duplicate it. That means you should have a strong grip on who your customer is and what she will buy. Your inventory should be under control and clean. The daily operations should be efficient. If your employees are falling over each other by the end of the day and you have work that has not been completed on time, you'd better get that straightened out before you duplicate your problems. In short, you must have a clear idea of your customer, a clean inventory, effective personnel, and efficient ordering practices.

Once things are in order, you can set up your new business plan. What do you expect from this expansion? How are you going to accomplish it? What is the time frame? How much will it cost? Consider ALL the related costs: new inventory, equipment, personnel, advertising, promotions, decorating, and general business expense. Good luck!

PERSONNEL

How often is it necessary to train or retrain employees?

A. Initial training obviously should be conducted within the first month of hiring a sales clerk, art consultant, or picture framer. However, we should not stop there. Retraining is often overlooked and, as a result, experienced staff are sometimes not up–to–date on the latest state–of–the–art techniques and technology. The need for retraining depends partly on the rate of change in the field. It may also be considered if you are expanding and offering more services or different types of products or as a matter of job enlargement or enrichment. Keep in mind that if employees are insufficiently trained, the business will suffer and they will be dissatisfied with their jobs.

I'd like to put together a couple of pages of information for new employees. Any suggestions?

A. To fit in with old employees, a new person needs to know working hours (are they expected to show up 10 minutes before the shop opens?), lunch arrangements, breaks, time–clock regulations and reporting absences. You may also want to include: clothing requirements or restrictions, pay schedules, sick–day provisions, parking instructions, insurance policies, employee discount details, and options for working on personal projects.

Outline this information in a booklet, and give it to new employees as a reference source. Even if your initial interview is long and detailed, few individuals can absorb all the pertinent information.

You may consider including an introduction to the company. Outline its history, goals, and a description of its products and services. It will help new employees explain it to their friends as well as to customers.

I have been paying my employees weekly. Each Friday they receive their pay for the prior week's work. I'd like to pay them biweekly because it will cut the payroll checks per employee from 52 to 26 and, therefore, save me a lot of time. How can I do this without making the employees wait another week?

A. This is not as difficult as it may seem. I did exactly this in my shop about 10 years ago. We may need a little illustration here. Let's set up a calendar for a sample month:

24	25	26	27	28	29	30
1	2	3	4	5	6	7
8	9	10	**11**	12	13	14
15	16	17	18	19	20	21
22	23	24	**25**	26	27	28

Your current paydays are the 6th, 13th, 20th, and 27th.

Instead of paying them on Friday, begin to pay them on Wednesday. The new paydays will be the 11th and the 25th. Instead of "holding" six days' pay, you will be holding pay for only three days.

To begin the process you will issue a check on the 6th for work done the 25th to the 30th. Then a check on the 11th for work the week of the 1st to the 7th. The next check will be for two weeks work from the 8th to the 21st and issued on the 25th.

Some of my salespeople like to wear designer blue jeans to work. I don't think blue jeans belong in business. Am I a stick–in–the–mud?

A. If you are a stick–in–the–mud, then so am I. Blue jeans have taken on an importance in some market areas and can be tolerated in certain stores. But jeans — no matter how expensive — are still casual apparel. What type of shop do you have? The clothing your salespeople wear reflects the image of your shop. I would not tolerate jeans or casual wear in my retail store. Perhaps you could suggest to your salespeople the type of clothing you expect them to wear. You also could provide solid color smocks or work aprons that would coordinate with the shop image.

Help! I have two full–time and two part–time employees. I am having a problem with tardiness. Do you think installing a time clock will cure this problem?

A. Tardiness is the result of management's inability to maintain control over its employees. As the owner or manager of the shop, you have to tell employees what is expected of them. Often, they think that if the store opens at 10 a.m. they only need to be there by 10 a.m. Explaining to them the need to arrive 10 minutes early probably will result in them arriving early. They simply do not know what is expected.

However, if someone is habitually late, there may be an underlying problem that neither you nor a time clock can fix. Time clocks do provide several benefits. With a time clock installed, you will have an accurate record of hours worked. You also will have a record of employees who make a constant effort to come in early. If you set up a time clock, set the rules at the time of installation. Each person must punch his or her time card only — no excuses, ever!

I am planning to hire two additional employees — one for the back room and another as a salesclerk/frame designer. I have had many artists apply for jobs here. Do you consider an art background very important?

A. A background in art would be helpful but is not necessary. I would be more concerned with personality and willingness to learn. The type of personality required of a person who will frame pictures all day, every day, is quite different from the type required for a salesperson. It has been my experience that the most productive worker in the back room is a quiet, methodical, detail–oriented person.

If applicants are artists, I look for one who works in pencil or pen and ink — or perhaps a jeweler. Someone who sees and removes a speck of dust also understands why nail holes must be placed properly and knows a tight corner when she sees one. Warning: If an artist has done her own picture framing, it will take you as much time to break her of her amateur ways as it does to train someone who is totally new to the field.

As for the salesperson, hire someone who likes to sell — an enthusiastic, happy, delighted–with–life type of person. This personality does not work well in the back room because people like this go crazy being cooped up. They need the action that goes on in the front room. Not everyone can sell art and framing comfortably. When training the salesperson, make sure she understands what goes into making both art and framing, even if she does not have to be able to do either — the salesperson must have respect for the processes. An understanding of the value of the product is very important to confident selling. If the salesperson feels the product is too expensive or unnecessary she will short change the customer by only showing the least expensive lines. Above all, before you hire someone, find out if she is color–blind and whether she understands fractions of an inch.

MANAGEMENT

I am having trouble with quality control. Our shop has fast turnover, and we handle a lot of goods daily: nothing too fancy — single and double mats, dry mounting, and fitting. The quality of the framing is fine — the problem lies with the handling of the customer's goods! The back room workers do not have the least bit of remorse when they damage something. Granted, most of the art is not high quality, but it has enough value for the customer to want to frame it. These mistakes are embarrassing, expensive, and time–consuming to correct. How can I get these people to care?

A. Apparently, the employees don't think there is anything wrong with the mistakes they have made. Somehow, they have come to believe that you don't mind, or the punishment for the crime isn't severe enough to make them be more careful. It is your job to train these people to handle the goods with respect.

Start with a meeting once a week until the problem is solved; thereafter, meetings may be held less often. All employees must attend so that everyone understands the importance and the goals of the company. Explain the company's position, and describe the new handling policies that will be maintained and monitored. Be very clear about how you want goods to be processed. Make a list and post it in the back room, near the lunch table, over the time clock and/or in the pay envelopes.

Go over each of the rules in the first meeting. Explain why the rules have been made. Ask for employee suggestions on how to stop the problems that have occurred. Perhaps you can liven up these lectures by showing videos on how art is made, such as the *Works of Art on Paper* videotape available from *DECOR*. Information like this will encourage your employees to respect the art they're handling. You will have to stress that no matter what is being framed, the framer is held responsible for its safety while it is in his or her possession.

Here are a few other suggestions for handling this problem:

1. Post signs around the workroom stating: "Handle customers' goods carefully — you are responsible!"
2. Outline specific policies for each procedure in the store so that when the staff changes, procedures do not. Have these procedures professionally lettered and hung on the wall in the back room or anywhere they are seen constantly.
3. Be careful that your own attitude isn't partially to blame. (Don't say things like "Look at this junk we have to frame.")
4. Schedule a series of half–hour training sessions showing how art is made; require all workers to be present.
5. Tell employees to put themselves in the customer's place and ask them, "How would you feel if this happened to you?"
6. If art is damaged, deduct its cost from the employee's wages.
7. Take away privileges.
8. Make the employee call the customer and tell him or her what happened to his or her art. This is the worst punishment of all — having to admit to a stranger that you have damaged his or her prop erty.

Help, this place is crazy! My frame shop and gallery is six years old. Business is good, but I work all the time and have four employees (two full–time and two part–time.) I don't have time for a day off and never seem to get control of this place. What am I doing wrong?

A. My guess is you started the shop by yourself and your company grew, so you added people every time things got overwhelming. You are the owner and manager of this business. You are in charge of the over–all business plan, setting the style and image of the shop, controlling expenses, and developing teamwork.

In order for the operation to run smoothly 90 percent of the time, each employee should have a special direction. If all employees are doing all the jobs, it is less efficient than designating jobs. I'm not suggesting an assembly line — just assigned areas of responsibility.

Since you are the owner/manager, you are responsible for planning, directing, controlling, evaluating, and adjusting the business. You should maintain overall business supervision (not by doing it all yourself) of buying, advertising, selling, inventory, displays, credits, deliveries, the office, personnel hiring, training, and firing.

Responsibilities for you to delegate to people in the sales area include: greeting customers, selling goods, keeping the store clean, updating displays, checking shipments that arrive at the front door and redirecting them, maintaining current prices, controlling cash (including petty cash) and tax-exempt slips, maintaining the mailing list, controlling inventory, and calling in orders for goods.

Designated responsibilities for employees in the back room include: completing framing orders on time, maintaining an inventory of framing materials, keeping equipment in good repair, and cleaning and organizing the work area.

Consider which employee is best suited to each job. Put him or her in charge of that task. Employees will be happy to have some responsibility that makes them feel more important to the company. A meeting once a month will be a good way to keep everything up to date.

You might also consider taking a course at your local college on small business management — it works and besides, you need the time off!

PRODUCTION

What sales volume can you expect to generate from a single framer working essentially full–time?

A. An experienced picture framer should be able to complete a job — cut the frame, glass, mat and filler board, join the frame and attach the artwork, seal it up and attach the wire — in 40 to 45 minutes. An inexperienced one should do it in an hour. Framers in my shop are doing 12 frames per day. There are practices that make some jobs go faster. In our shop we use something called a sandwich fit. We fit all the pieces of a frame at one time, tape all the edges to keep dust from getting in, then put it aside and go to the next one. We also have one person who cuts and joins frames, another who does fitting and assembly, and so on.

How about an assistant? When the store is really busy, especially around the holiday season, the assistant can come in an hour early and get everything ready for the framer to work on. Why waste the time of an experienced framer? Let the assistant find a sheet of *Cameo Rose* and gather the parts required for the frame job.

We have two full–time framers, and two salespeople help out when it is not busy in the front of the store. We are making about 25 to 30 frames per week and never seem to get caught up. How many frame jobs can you expect a framer to complete each day?

A. Eight to fifteen. A time study organized by the PPFA in 1979 indicates it should take 35 to 45 minutes to: complete a job of cutting and joining wood moulding; cut a mat, a piece of glass and filler board; and seal with dust cover and screw eyes.

Certainly, there are many variables, but it does give a base from which to operate. Obviously, more complicated jobs, such as shadow boxes and large tapestries, will take longer; however, they will be more than balanced with 8x10" photo frames and simple fitting jobs.

Take a time study in your own shop. It will give you a guide of what to expect from your framers. Two full–time uninterrupted framers should be able to process 60 to 80 frames per week.

The workers will perform better if they know what is expected from them. If you don't have a full–day's work for a given day, fill it with samples for the store — framed art to sell, ready–made frames and mats — keep them busy!

We have been using a "grocery list" style of work order form. I've had difficulty getting my sales people to check the correct boxes and fill in the form properly. They usually scribble across the face of it. What can I do to get them to fill in the form?

A. I would streamline the form, listing only the jobs that are performed most often — frame, glass, mat, mounting, and fitting. Leave room on the form for small descriptive drawings and pertinent measurements. Most importantly, train your salespeople to use the form and make it quite clear what you expect them to do. Besides the obvious information, I make sure my salespeople record the name and phone number of *every* customer, the date, the initials of the salesperson, perfect measurements, and clear, concise instructions so that any framer can complete the job without consulting the salesperson.

GALLERY

If a manufacturer or publisher wants you to locate an artist who does a certain type of work, how is a "finder's fee" arranged? Who pays? How do I determine the amount of the fee?

A. Sorry, there's no rule book to cover this one. After several phone calls to publishers, I found no specific arrangements. One paid 10 percent of the purchase price of the rights to publish (which generally is not very high). Some paid a flat fee of $50, $100, $200, etc. Most paid nothing, except for a "thank you." If you became the artists' agent, you could collect a portion of the royalties.

How does a gallery secure the investment of limited editions? Who decides what the cost will be and when to raise the cost of an edition — especially when the edition may be in other galleries in the area or state?

A. Dealing with a reputable publisher helps to keep the prices balanced. Other galleries may decide to price their limited editions differently from yours — higher or lower — and you are unable to change that. It's the American way. I don't really think a gallery can secure the value of limited editions. The publisher/artist will decide on the cost. When the edition is sold out, the publisher may list the price as higher. It is the public that will put the real value on it. If they want it, how much are they willing to pay for it? It's idle speculation to predict the future of a limited edition print. Only time will tell if it will keep its intrinsic value as a work of art, as well as its high market value.

I am looking for information concerning how to market limited edition reproductions. What should I buy? How can I tell if the market is saturated?

A. Several limited edition publishers have advice on marketing their products. They provide catalogues, tear sheets, and ads to use to get interest from customers.

Your question on *what* to buy is really tough. If you've established a style to your gallery and you carry types of prints that will fit in with your style, you'll be much better off than if you try to buy every style available.

You'll know when you've saturated the market when your customers stop buying. Perhaps after a few years of experience in this field you'll be better able to read the signals and can tell when that is about to happen. Merchandising is a fine art in itself.

Why are limited edition reproductions more popular than open editions? What are the pricing considerations?

A. They are not necessarily more popular — in sheer numbers open editions sell many times more than limited editions. There is the prestige and pride of ownership in hanging a piece of artwork that is available only in limited numbers. Value is another consideration. To be considered valuable, a piece will have the combination of rareness, importance of image, standing of the artist, and quality of the work.

The pricing will reflect these considerations — along with the fact that the artist will have spent many years studying, plus the time spent in creating the single painting from which the edition will be made. There is also the cost of printing, color separations, paper quality, and support materials to help market the limited edition print on the retail level.

What are the obligations of a gallery owner to a consignee regarding damage, loss, or theft of consigned art?

A. While the work of art has been placed in your care, you are responsible for it. You would have to make restitution. There are many ways of working with artists. A book I used in setting up some of the arrangements is *What Every Artist & Collector Should Know About The Law*, by Scott, Hodes, Dutton & Co.

Is the best way to sell limited edition prints through a catalog or to carry the inventory? If through a catalog, is it professional to ask for prepayment of 50 percent?

A. The best way to sell limited edition prints is framed — and well framed at that. The second best way is to have them in bins or shelving units. You have to treat limited edition prints as special — or anything you sell, for that matter. Just putting them into folders hoping your customers will recognize their value is asking for a lot of imagination. That is why framing is so important to the sale of any artwork. Don't be afraid to decide how something should be framed — you are the expert.

Your customer does not know how many different ways a print could be framed. You, on the other hand, have several ideas for special treatment of a print. If because of limited display space you are able to frame only a few, then you will have to stock the remainder in bins or drawers. Be careful of this method; you can build a large inventory and have a hard time selling it. You will have to spend a great deal of time showing your customer the artwork and explaining the artistic value of the piece when it is "just" in the bin.

The third way to sell limited edition prints is to use catalogs. Catalogs are excellent backup sales tools. They also show the customer that the artist is "legitimate" — being in print looks very important; however, using a catalog can be very confusing and you, of course, have to deal with ordering the print, which may be out of print already. Should you ask for a down payment? Definitely! Half of the price is not out of the question.

Many customers want to exchange graphics when they change their decor. Sometimes they have had the artwork for five years or more. How do most galleries handle such requests?

A. If it is simply a piece of decorative art, it is the same as an out of style accessory or a piece of used furniture. If you are talking about a very valuable piece perhaps worth thousands of dollars, you might like to take it back to sell on the secondary market or in your store. It is difficult for customers to understand that you buy art at wholesale and sell it at retail prices. Explain that you can take it back only if the piece is worth considerably more than the original purchase price and only if there is a market for it. You can take a percentage of the selling price as your fee and commission for selling the piece.

If you have a piece framed in your gallery and you have a person who will buy it if it's framed differently, how do you charge for it?

A. Well, I would take the print out and sell the customer the print at its regular price and add the price of the new framing A lot of us think we've wasted our time on the first framing. But we'll find something else to put in that framing unit, and we'll put it back on the wall for sale.

At one time in our gallery, we were quite snooty about that sort of thing and said, "No, after all we have time invested in this and we picked out this framing. You should use it." But then we got desperate for sales. There is no more arrogant framing in our store.

What if the customer just wants the print without the frame?

A. Sell it. Hey, you're a retailer; you need the money. Use the frame immediately for another picture or a mirror.

What is the mortality rate of new galleries going into business?

A. I could not find specific statistics for galleries; however, a call to the Economic Development Board of Ohio gave me some interesting data — 1.5 out of 10 new business will succeed. That's looking on the positive side. The mortality rate is 85 percent!

Dun & Bradstreet studied the demise of 12,000 businesses and found that 49 percent failed because of incompetence. Scary, isn't it? There are some things you can do to lessen the risk of failure.

1. *Learn about how a business is run.* Pick up a book on retailing or on starting a small business.

2. *Take a course provided locally by the Small Business Administration.* The courses are usually condensed and to the point.

3. *Work for someone who already has that type of business to learn the basics.*

4. *Make sure that you understand bookkeeping.* Bookstores offer instructional books and tapes or your local Continuing Education programs should help. You will need to know as much about business as you do about art — more!

The lack of planning is one of the most frequently cited reasons for business failures. Business persons, especially sole proprietors and other small business owners, are usually so preoccupied with daily crisis and putting out fires that they have neither time nor inclination to plan and look ahead. You should have a very specific plan that would outline why, how and when you will achieve profitability.

What are some ideas on how an artist should approach gallery owners with his work?

A. You'll need a brochure with information about yourself. A biography including education and awards should accompany photos or slides of your work. If you mail the information include a self-addressed envelope for return of the slides. If you intend on a personal visit, call for an appointment.

Include price, availability, and quantity of the work along with how you can be reached. Define the procedures the gallery owner should take if interested in purchasing or consigning your work. Gallery owners are reluctant to deal with artists who do not approach their art in a businesslike manner.

What steps are possible to break a stranglehold a single gallery has on all popular and not-so-popular local artists? All artists are under contract with this gallery. In a town of over 100,000, should there not be room for competition?

A. It depends on the town and its economic condition. This gallery sounds as though it has been operating successfully for the artists it represents. I will guess that it has made these artists popular through its marketing and promotion. The artists have gone to this gallery because it is the only one in town or it is the most successful. You have two options: 1) seek and develop your own stable of artists — it will take time and a lot of promotion for both your gallery and the artists; 2) steal the artists from the existing gallery — you will have to consider what it will take to have them leave and join your gallery. Artists are looking for promotion and sales and having both lead to fame and fortune (the starving artist routine is strictly for TV).

The older gallery probably has established a name in the community, a following, and a good track record. It takes time to develop these. Perhaps you could study the market and see if there are areas in art that are left unserved — the contemporary market, etchings, antique art, limited edition prints, or watercolors. Certainly there are more artists in your city that are not exhibiting in the other gallery and, of course, there are always new artists to nurture and much undiscovered talent waiting to be recognized. Eventually, you will develop your own style gallery with your own stable of artists.

For galleries in high tourist areas, what percentage of traffic is local vs. tourist traffic? What percentage of original art is sold to the tourists?

A. Not having a gallery dependent on the tourist trade, I had to poll several galleries to get answers, or should I say questions for you. By answering the following questions, you will get a better understanding of what to expect. Sorry, there are no across–the–board percentages to pass along. And your question about original art would be totally up to the type of gallery, meaning the type of stock a gallery has to sell.

Perhaps the following questions will help you to analyze your situation: Is the tourism seasonal? Is there more than one shopping area? Do the residents shop where the tourists shop? Do the residents have a gallery in the normal shopping area? Is what you sell so unique they must buy it from you?

The consensus is that residents do not mix with the tourists if there is a choice of shopping centers. The natives prefer to stay away from "the maddening crowd." I can vouch for that! I lived in Niagara Falls for 23 years and never went into the downtown area until after "they" were gone. The majority of my shopping was done in areas that served the residents, generally with lower prices than what the tourist industry needs to survive.

We've had our gallery for two years. Should we offer leasing or rental artwork?

A. There is a great difference between leasing and renting. If you rent a framed piece, you can charge any amount over a period of time, under conditions to which the customer agrees. The IRS does not have any rulings on rentals. As far as the IRS is concerned, you own the property, you pay the tax on the asset, and you can charge people to look at it. However, when it comes to leasing the IRS is concerned that it be handled correctly. The IRS may wonder: Who really owns this property? How much is this really worth? Who is paying the taxes? What is the true value of the piece? Is the lease just another method of purchasing? Is this lease in any way devised to avoid taxation? Should this property increase in value, who will pay the additional tax and when? Yes, it can get very complicated.

You may choose to have a third party handle your leases since the laws change frequently. Leasing can be used as a selling tool for large purchases of $2,000 or more but is not effective for lesser–priced items. It may be easier just to set up a payment plan for your customer.

I've heard of galleries that allow pieces to go out on approval. How does that work? What do you do if the pieces are damaged?

A. Selling on approval is a very successful method of selling art. Someone is attracted to a piece in your shop, but she is not sure. Besides, her husband is out of town and he would have to see it, but he won't be back until next week. I bet you've heard that one before. Selling on approval will do away with all the inane excuses and probably sell the customer more than she originally planned.

Here's how it works. The customer likes several pieces but has reservations — too small, too pink, too costly, etc. You suggest she take them out on approval, because it is the only way she can get the real feeling from the art. This way she can see how the pieces will fit in her home. After all, she will live with them a long time, and the effect they will have in her living room is as important as her choice of couch or carpet. It is very important to us as dealers that she be in love with her new choice.

Now you explain how approval works. She need only to leave a signed credit card slip or check for the amount — you will not put the card through unless she instructs you to. You will hold the credit card slip or check while she decides (three or four days) and then call her to see how she likes the pieces. We do encourage the customer to take more than one — perhaps three different pieces; if she's decorating, she'll find room for the others. We have been selling on approval for more than eight years and have had only two pieces damaged. We absorb the cost — a small price to pay for the number of sales generated.

We have a customer who would like to sell an original oil painting by a famous living artist. This painting was appraised at $65,000 a year ago. Could you give us any tips on marketing it?

A. Here are a few suggestions:

1. Since this artist is still living and famous, he undoubtedly is represented by an agent or a gallery. Find that gallery, and tell the owner what you have. The best scenario is that the gallery already will have built up a

market for the piece and probably will have willing and ready customers. For making the arrangements, you and the representing gallery each should receive a commission against the sale price.

2. Photograph the piece on slide film, and send the slide to major auction galleries listed in the Yellow Pages of metropolitan cities.

3. Invite "important" customers — the ones with "real money" — to a private showing of the piece.

4. Take out advertisements in local papers.

5. Build a show or promotion around the piece. Use the painting as a theme, and display other artwork having similar style or subject matter. Visitors who admire the original but cannot afford it might buy similar art or reproductions.

Remember, you cannot make a poster print of the original to sell, unless you have permission from both the artist and the representing gallery

We have had customers request an appraisal of their art "collection." We have only been in business for four months. How do we do this?

A. This request is faced by framers and gallery store owners daily. It is a delicate situation. Specific knowledge of the type of art, as well as its value in the economic art world, is required. Appraising a limited edition print that was published in the past 10 years would be easy; simply contact the publisher (many publishers are listed in *DECOR*'s annual Sources Directory. If the art is an oil painting "that has been in the family for many generations" and the customer considers it valuable — this is a tough one! It may simply be a painting done by Aunt Mary.

If the artist was a significant artist of his time and there is a demand for his work, it will be easier to trace. However, the painting could be an 1875 version of a $29.95 over–the–sofa painting or simply a nice painting that Aunt Mary did while taking classes at the community center.

Value is based on importance of the artist, rareness, condition, and appeal. Without knowledge of historical art values and prices, it may be difficult to identify a truly valuable piece from Aunt Mary's painting. Of course, it may be that Aunt Mary's last name was Cassatt, in which case, documentation will be easier to obtain.

Here are a few suggestions that may help you.

The public library is a great source of information. There are reference books that record the selling prices of artwork. These are often grouped by time period or subject matter, such as western, American or Eastern European.

The large auction houses, such as Sotheby's and Christie's, maintain catalogs of collections. Some of these catalogs may be purchased. If you are confident the artwork is significant, send a slide of it to one of the auction houses — they would be interested and may be able to provide some information.

Check out old print catalogs and price sheets, as well as old issues of *DECOR* magazine, for any clue. Your local museum may be able to provide information, especially on significant local artists.

There is a national association of appraisers who specialize in different categories of art. The local chapter of the American Society of Appraisers may be in the Yellow Pages, or write to the American Society of Appraisers, P.O. Box 17265, Washington, DC 20041.

For artwork produced in the past 20 years, you may be able to track down the printer, artist, or representative gallery that could provide you with the current value of the piece. There are also several source books and software programs available that provide historical and current prices for limited editions.

Perhaps there is an art dealer in town who has developed this type of knowledge and could sort out the common from the outstanding.

Do not hesitate to charge for the research you will undertake to get this information. How much? Keep track of your time, and charge accordingly.

We have had a custom frame shop for four years and are just going to add a gallery. We have had requests from our customers for limited edition art. How much should I buy, and what kind of art should I purchase?

A. The amount spent on inventory to get started will have a direct relationship on the amount of revenue. An investment (a key word here) of $10,000 net initial inventory with continual restocking should bring in $50,000 in retail sales per year and still leave you with a base inventory.

As for what type of artwork you should invest in — this is a very important decision. You could have original Rembrandts available for $100 and if your customer does not like them, you will not sell them. What types of limited art have your customers requested? Do you think you can sell that kind of art to others? Limited edition art is available in as many subjects as posters and reproductions. You may want to choose an area of specialty, such as country, wildlife, or contemporary prints. Notice the type of work brought in by your customers. Consider their taste in art and framing when you make this decision. When you shop at a trade show, don't just breeze through the aisles. Study the exhibits for trends. Don't forget the price range — what are your customers willing to spend?

The art you purchase may be a smattering of various subjects and media to see how it is accepted by customers in your area. Or you may have decided what subjects and media you are comfortable with — great! Just make sure your customers will like it, too. It is all very good to buy treasured art and frame it beautifully, but the difference between a retail art gallery and a museum is that the museum doesn't want to sell the work that hangs on it — and a gallery must sell its art!

Where can I learn about the art publishing business? What kind of information can you give me on the risk/return on various distribution systems such as trade shows, direct mail, magazine advertising, sales reps, displays in merchandise marts, and so on?

I would like to form my own company to publish the works of artists who have a future. How much money do I need to start out? How do I contact these artists? Are there specific guidelines to follow? What books should I read?

A. Since these two questions are so closely related, I'll give an answer that covers both.

Like any business, art publishing has its own unique risks and rewards. But it is a business and, as such, follows certain basic guidelines. General information is available in the business section of the public library, where you can find many books that cover the subjects of manufacturing, representation, distribution, marketing, selling wholesale, selling retail, and so on.

There are two areas of business that you must learn: general business operating procedures and the art publishing field. Experience is always the best teacher, but when you don't have it, you can get help from a consultant or someone who has been in the field. A knowledgeable person can save you from years of mistakes and possible failure.

One excellent source of information about the art industry is *Art Marketing Handbook* by Calvin J. Goodman (available from *DECOR*). Goodman is a consultant specializing in the art field. This book, which is very thorough and covers all phases in the art business, is the best I have read on this topic.

Success in any business relies on three things: knowledge, need, and capital.

You must have knowledge about the specific industry you're interested in as well as an understanding of the day–to–day operations of the business itself. When a company fails, it is often because it was run by an individual who lacked management and business–operating experience.

It is also difficult for a business to succeed unless there is a need for its product or service, or at least the opportunity to develop such a need. If no one really wants the product or the market is already serviced, it won't matter how great the product is; no one will buy it.

As for capital — sure, I know, you will never have enough money; however, many failures can be attributed directly to the fact that those who started the business ignored or underestimated the need for adequate financing. To start a business on bare bones is to doom it before it starts.

MERCHANDISING

We're in a new shop, and we've purchased some of the inexpensive posters (under $50). How do other shops frame these? A $10 or $20 poster hardly merits a $50 to $100 frame job. Yet because of the poster size, it's almost impossible to custom frame them for less. We haven't found any other way to save the customer much money. Is this a problem with other shops, and how do they handle it?

A. All frame shops have this problem. The cost or value of the work to be framed has no relation to the cost of time and materials that go into custom framing. Here are some less expensive methods:

1. Dry mount the poster on a foam–centered board and put a sticky hanger on the back.
2. Dry mount it and wrap the poster in shrink wrap, also using a sticky hanger.
3. Dry mount it, glass it, and use a clip style frame that holds everything together with four corner clips.
4. Buy one style of metal section frame in bulk to keep the price down.

There also are several brackets available within our industry that may provide the support without a regular frame. Do not underestimate the value of the poster to the customer. Just because the print only cost $20 doesn't mean that the customer doesn't want it to look like it cost $120. If you're trying to compete with mass production companies and importers, you can't. Unless, of course, you start that kind of business. Remember, the lamp always costs more than the light bulb.

My staff is continually arguing over the type of music we play in the shop. Should I just get rid of it completely?

A. The music that is played in any shop is part of the image of the store. What type of image do you want to project? The choice of music is very important and should be made by the owners — and employees should understand this.

Customers must feel comfortable in a shop. The music being played as a background "filler" should not be noticeable. You do not want to offend anyone or make anyone anxious to leave. When a customer comes into your shop to browse, he may feel awkward if he is the only customer. He may feel you are watching him or can hear every move he makes. This is where the music will "fill" the spaces and cover the awkward silences.

As popular as rock music is, it still annoys a certain segment of society, and I can't take a chance with any of my customers. I prefer "elevator" music or classical — very quietly.

Has direct mail retailing of oils on a consumer level been done before?

A. Several phone calls to wholesalers produced the answer "No." It appears you have a unique idea. Concerns voiced by the wholesalers were mainly in cataloguing and shipping. If more than one painting of a particular scene is available, how can you explain that to a customer? Will the paintings be shipped flat, rolled, or stretched? Will they be available framed? Can you get repeat sales? It looks like a tough product for direct mail; however, the success of direct mail marketing for so many other products may have paved the way. Nothing ventured, nothing gained.

We are looking for marketing ideas for our hardwood frames that are suitable for photo art and posters. Our 1–1/2" birch frame, 16x20, sells for less than $3 in two finishes. Our production volume is 2,500 per week.

A. Marketing is the key word. The answer to your dilemma may be found by answering several questions. How do you want to sell this product? Retail? Wholesale? Do you want to sell the frames empty or complete with artwork? Do you want to sell them individually, by the dozen, by the pallet, or by the truck or train car? Where is your market — your key customer? Here are several possible ways to sell this product:

1. You, as the producer, could sell to a distributor, who may sell the goods in smaller quantities to his/her customer — the retailer.

2. You could sell your product to a wholesaler who will change your product — add artwork or repackage — for the photo or gift industry. This

wholesaler will promote these goods to the dealer, who in turn promotes to the retail customer.

3. You could hire sales representatives to sell your product, as is, to the retail dealer.

4. You could sell direct to the customer, which means you open retail space or sell via mail order.

Wholesalers, distributors, and dealers can be found within our trade by advertising in trade journals, by phone calls, through direct mail, by contacting sales representatives, and at trade shows and conventions. Names of companies can be found in the Sources Directory published by *DECOR* each July and in publications from the Professional Picture Framers Association (PPFA), the National Art Materials Trade Association (NAMTA), and the Professional Photographers Association (PPA).

Our current frame corner display consists of 950 samples, of which 650 are wood and the remainder are aluminum. In addition to our gallery and frame shop, we rent a building that contains our length inventory and chopping equipment. We have approximately 100 various mouldings in inventory. The money we save on length vs. chop does not justify the expense of the chop shop. What are some ways to improve this situation?

A. Most framers stock in length the profiles that sell the best — no trendy styles — just the classics. Perhaps you could stock 50 to 100 mouldings and back that up with 300 chop corners. Anything over 400 is a lot of duplication or a lot of trendy styles. Reduce the corner samples to between 400 and 500, and reduce the number of companies you deal with so you have significant orders to place with three or four companies, thereby reducing ordering costs, meeting minimums and becoming more important to those companies. When you deal with 10 different companies, you are not likely to have the volume of orders to become an important customer or to get the best prices.

Other problems associated with huge displays of corner samples are: The designer/salesperson has to cover a lot of territory to get the correct corner for each job. The customer is overwhelmed — a first time framing customer doesn't know which one is the least expensive, so she has you price them all. The regular customer will take the salesperson's suggestion, which probably comes from among the salespersons 10 favorite mouldings.

Many corner samples are underpriced or have been discontinued because of the chore of updating so many samples. When mispriced or unavailable mouldings remain on the wall, orders are written, resulting in wasted time and lost profits.

You do need representation of each moulding group. Manufacturers tend to specialize in a particular moulding group, such as low– to middle–price stains and painted finishes, high polish furniture finishes, and the gold and silver finishes on period frames. Have a supplier for each of these moulding groups, then add a metal moulding supplier, and you're covered. If you have the entire line of corner samples from each company, you do not have to display each sample. Choose a representative selection, and stock the balance in the back room. You can get them if you absolutely have to find something else for a customer.

If you can deal with a local distributor, you may pay a penny more a foot, but it's worth it to have selection and speedy service without stocking everything.

Here are the major differences between chop and length:

CHOP — Traditional markup is three to four times the wholesale cost of the moulding, including the freight. Freight can be a significant cost, especially if it is COD. If you are in a remote area, delivery may not be fast. There is no inventory, no storage necessary, and no waste. Large orders usually can be switched to a purchase of length moulding. Only assembling, not cutting, equipment is required. Since no order is placed until the product is sold, every purchase yields a 100 percent sale.

LENGTH — Traditional markup is five to six times the wholesale price, including the freight. Freight is proportionately less for bundles than chops. There is waste (even if you make mini frames someday!) and the risk that the moulding may not sell. More capital is needed to purchase, store, cut, and assemble. And you need more equipment and employees to maintain and sell length.

So which choice is better? Depending on your present situation — number of trained employees, amount of space, and money for investment — you may choose all length, all chop or a combination of both.

I have some really nice limited edition prints that haven't sold. I have put them on sale, and they still haven't sold. Some of these prints have been around for many years. What am I doing wrong?

A. Basically, it is a marketing problem. The product must be keyed to the customer. The print may be under– or overpriced, or it may be the wrong color, image, or size. Style is very important to art.

How long can you afford to keep these prints? Why are you keeping them? With any prints, you have to ask yourself, "Are they in demand?" If so, they should sell right away. If your prints haven't sold, why haven't they?

Are you buying artwork for your customer or for yourself? Your taste in art may not sell. I'm not saying it is good or bad taste — just that your selections may not sell to your present customers.

Pay more attention to your customer's requests — her likes and dislikes. Have promotions to educate customers to understand the quality of your products. There is a short video available from *DECOR* called *Works of Art on Paper* that explains the various printing processes. This can be shown in the shop — it only runs 20 minutes. Use it as a promotion, and get people involved.

Use a local artist/printmaker to display work and possibly show photographs of the printing process. This will help the customer place a greater value on this type of work and encourage purchases.

How do I inquire about the top selling posters? I am testing my market, but I could use some help.

A. Dealing with a company that can send a sales representative to call on you would be the safest bet. The salesperson is interested in making sales and knows which posters or prints are selling. She or he will be glad to tell you which are the hottest ones. But be careful. As with anything, popularity depends on the subject matter, color, and timing. Poster images go in and out of style and you may saturate your market with a certain image. Keep testing your market — that process never stops.

Vivian, what is your average turn on artwork?

A. I try to turn the inventory four times per year — three at least. If I haven't sold a print in six months, I know I've made a mistake — the wrong price, size, color, or image. I'm pretty much convinced I'm going to keep it. I'll then give it as a gift to the public service TV station and let them auction it off on television and make myself look good. If it hasn't moved in three months, we move it around the store or maybe reframe it.

By the way, when you donate things only donate good stuff. Don't donate the really junky stuff, because your name goes on it.

I'll have half–price sales when I no longer want to keep my inventory as an investment. A poster is not going to get higher priced. So I try to move things out quickly.

What about wood moulding that doesn't seem to move anymore?

A. "Anymore?" It sounds as if it is out of style. Mark it down right away! The $6 moulding becomes a $3 discontinued moulding — and what a bargain for your "sale" conscious customer. If you still can't get rid of it — cut it up into ready–mades.

What do you do with pictures on the wall that are damaged or that you can't sell? What do you do with frames that you've cut too short?

A. Distressed stock in our business should be handled very much the way it's handled in other retail stores. You've been in a clothing store that has a dress that's gone out of style. First, it goes on sale; then it becomes a bargain; then it's gone. It disappears. Did the owners find someone to buy it? Maybe. Maybe not. But they got rid of it.

You have to use standard retail practices to get rid of your stock. I know it hurts a lot when you pay $100 for something and you have to sell it for $5. You tend to think if you discount something 10%, it's a big deal. But would *you* walk across the street for a 10% off sale? No. It's 50% or forget it. Distressed goods normally go for 10 to 20 percent of normal retail price, and if you can find someone who'll pay that, you're doing fine.

Pictures that do not sell? These are mistakes — wrong size, color, subject matter, or price for your customer. Trade with another gallery and/or frameshop, give to the goodwill, give them to your family — do not give them as door prizes — do you want a mistake to represent your company?

Mistake frames? Find artwork to fit. Put a mirror in it. Turn it into a ready–made size. Mistake moulding? Say you've got walnut moulding with an avocado panel. You're waiting for this to come back in style — green should be stylish in the 90s. But you have to wait for avocado *and* dark Mediterranean woods to come back in — you're asking for a lot here. Cut it up into ready–mades. Change its color; sell it to someone else; put an ad in the classifieds — but dump the stuff. If you maintain inventory and keep building it up, you are going nowhere. You're only building up dead money.

This frame shop is two years old. We use 80 percent chop service, have a few ready-mades, and stock 30 mouldings that we cut on the chopper. We are making about 20 to 40 frames per week. We ask the customers to call us in two to three weeks for pickup instructions. They don't seem to mind calling us, and it saves us time calling them. Is two-to-three-week turnaround reasonable?

A. No. One week is acceptable turnaround time; two weeks is for special projects; three weeks — you are just putting off the work. The longer customers wait, the less enthusiastic they are about picking up things. When customers bring in pieces, they are excited and "can't wait" to pick them up. Three weeks later, they barely remember what they brought in.

From a practical standpoint, having a piece in your shop for an extended period of time increases the chance of it getting damaged, lost, or forgotten. The longer the wait — the longer you have to wait for the money.

A customer should not have to call to find out if an item is ready. At the time she leaves the order, give her a completion date, perhaps one or two weeks from the day she brings it in. Tell her you will *not* be calling her unless there is a question about the project.

What should I do with inventory that does not sell? I don't think it's right to mark down original artwork, and I don't know how to explain to the customer that the limited edition print I sold her in September is on sale in my gallery for a lower price now that it's December.

A. That customer, in her lifetime, has seen markdowns on many, many, products — shoes, clothing, appliances and, the best one, jewelry — just a few days after she paid full price.

This is life; this is retail! Retailers provide goods and services for the going price at the time the customer wants or needs them.

Markdowns are as natural to retail as markups. The real problem with markdowns is that the retailer, when setting original prices, does not take into account the fact that all goods do not sell at the premium price.

Markdowns result from seven factors common to all retailers — including art dealers and custom framers:

1. Buying mistakes — goods not suited to your customers' needs. Ask

yourself: if the limited edition print did not sell when it was new and "hot," what are its chances after eight months?
2. *Pricing mistakes* — overpricing or underpricing, considering your competition and your customers' needs.
3. *Decline in wholesale price* — which means you're stuck with the expensive stuff.
4. *New, improved goods* — items that should replace those presently occupying your limited wall and storage space.
5. *Special promotions* — limited–time specials to build traffic.
6. *Overselling* — pursuing the "hard sell" with an unlikely customer, resulting in returns or goods not being picked up.
7. *Accumulation* — odds and ends, shopworn goods, and any seasonal items, all of which must be sold to maintain inventory control.

Markdowns do attract thrifty buyers, do result in impulse sales, and do keep inventory fresh. If you just can't bring yourself to mark down a fine work of art, consider major retailers such as Saks Fifth Avenue, Lord and Taylor, Neiman–Marcus, even Tiffany's. For years, these retailers have marked down items — but have advertised them as "special values" and "rare opportunities."

I have a chance to buy a lot of moulding from a distributor who is going out of business. I will be able to buy it at half the price he paid for it, but I have to buy all 14,000 feet of mixed patterns. My store presently uses mostly chops, and I buy 25 to 40 patterns in length. This purchase will allow me to be very competitive. Should I buy the moulding?

A. I can answer your question with several questions of my own:

1. How many patterns will you get?

2. How old is this stock? Old moulding is not a bargain. It dries up and goes out of style. When you look over the mouldings, seriously consider which ones are losers. Subtract those from the total footage you are buying; then recalculate the bargain. Eight hundred feet of lime–green moulding may be hard to move.

3. Will your employees be able to sell these mouldings?

4. Is the quality suitable for your shop?

5. Do you have room to store this much additional stock?

6. How many frames do you presently sell per week? This will di-

rectly affect how long it would take you to use 14,000 feet of moulding. If the average frame uses six feet of moulding, you will have bought enough moulding to make 2,333 frames.

When you say this purchase will enable you to be more competitive, are you referring to your prices? When pricing this moulding for retail, you must take into account the cost of waste, storage, and the interest rate on the money used for the purchase.

Keeping stock on hand is expensive. It ties up valuable storage space and useful money. Inventory can be a big cash trap. Each $100 in materials in storage can cost between $15 and $25 per year in handling, storage space, debt service, deterioration, taxes, and obsolescence.

I'm sure you can buy this moulding and give your customers some great prices, or even use it to make a bunch of ready–mades. Just balance your savings against the cash that will be tied up in inventory.

At tax inventory time, I was again perplexed by the same question I face each year. What is the value of a 4 ft. piece of moulding or half sheet of mat board? Like most framers, I'm afflicted with "Chronic Saver's Syndrome." I have accumulated a lot of end pieces of moulding that won't match new stock. Of course, I'm waiting for an 8x10" order of that moulding, or I plan to cut it up into ready–made frames in my spare time! Tax–wise, I'd be better off throwing it away than attempting to set a value on it.

A. The tax department would like you to be consistent. Whatever method you employ to record the value of your inventory should remain the same from year to year.

A popular method is: If you have less than 4' of moulding, a full sheet of mat board or a full lite of glass, do not count the items as inventory for tax purposes. These are scraps. They have no value. They are waste from manufacturing a product, for which you have charged a price that included a waste factor.

If that wondrous moment arrives when you actually do use the scraps and turn them into a project to sell, you will have an asset. If you sell the asset, you will collect sales tax and then pay taxes on the profits. Isn't the free enterprise system great?

CUSTOMER RELATIONS

What do I do with the customer who says, "Just looking"?

A. I suspect "just looking" is a response to "Can I help you?" How often have you been approached by a salesperson with that question? And what was your response? I bet you said, "Just looking" also. "Just looking" really means, "Hey, give me a break! I just got in the door and I don't even know what you have here, much less if I want to buy anything."

Whether the customer has come in to pick up a framed piece or to look around for hours, you will get more information with a simple acknowledgment of his or her existence. Try one of the following: "Hi," "Hello" or "Good morning." After customers realize that you know they exist, they will tell you what they want — *if* they know at that time.

Should you get a mumbled response, that is your clue to talk to them about the shop. "We have ready–mades over here and photo frames over there. Take your time and look around." Walk away and do something. Don't stand over their shoulders; look busy. After a period of time, walk by customers and say, "I almost forgot to show you this new item," or start a conversation about the artwork they are standing in front of.

And for art's sake, when a customer says she likes something, start to sell it! Don't confuse her with more stock or say, "This is the LAST one left" (which means the best one's are gone). Continue to talk about the artwork to find out what a customer likes and dislikes about the piece. During the conversation, you can mention that you take major credit cards, will change a mat color or moulding, deliver, or let her have it on approval. Help your customer make the decision with your expert guidance. Don't ask the customer if you can help — just do it!

My average sale in our frame shop is $75. How can I get it higher?

A. To increase the average sale, you have to sell higher–priced goods or additional goods to each customer. Your salespeople will have control over this area. In one–to–one selling, which is what we have in our frameshops, there are two people who influence the decision to buy and how much the sale will be — the customer and the salesperson.

First, the salesperson must understand the value of what he or she is selling. If that salesperson has never had anything custom framed or has expressed an opinion on how expensive custom framing is — there's going to be a problem. It will be very difficult for a salesperson to convince a customer of the value of conservation framing if he or she doesn't think it's necessary. The best way to help the salesperson upgrade is training. Explain to your sales staff why the services of the shop are valuable. Show them the different finishes available in moulding and the difference a quality finish or good wood makes. There are many price lines in furniture and many price lines in framing. Not all customers are looking for the economy model. Some want to buy the top of the line; they just don't want to be overcharged. Each person puts different values on goods. As long as the customer sees the value for the price paid, he or she is happy.

Let your salespeople know that you expect them to sell, not just take orders. Find people to work for you who want to sell rather than stand around waiting for the customer to make all of the decisions. The salespeople shouldn't be overly aggressive, but they should exert some influence on the sale. You may want to pay your sales staff a percentage of each sale to increase their desire to sell more. Don't forget to have some extra things, like small photo frames for snapshots and photographs, to sell to your customers. You may think pre–made photo frames are expensive compared to what you could make yourself, but you must look at how fast they will sell and how they are presented. These frames are already boxed with both easel back and hanger for the wall. People like the convenience and buy them on impulse. If you don't think they sell, look in your closest department store, drug store, or 5 & 10. They sell like crazy.

We offer conservation framing in our shop, but it takes so much time to explain it to the customer that we often skip it and sell them ordinary framing. Is there a shortcut we can use?

A. Education! A display on conservation framing will save you a lot of explaining. The display should show examples of damage caused by acidic mats and filler boards, insects, incorrect adhesives, excessive heat, and humidity. Use a piece of foam center board and create a "science fair project." If you don't have any examples of damaged pieces, you could pick up several at the local antique store. Then, of course, it should state that YOUR shop can help control this type of damage to customer's personal pieces. The more your customer understands about conservation methods, the easier it will be to sell. Having a display to point to will also help with any understanding and credibility problems.

Selling conservation framing to my customers is such a time–consuming project. Explaining to each customer the effects of acid boards and why we use rag board and Japanese paper hinges takes 45 minutes or more. It seems like the more you explain, the more you have to explain! I still want to offer conservation framing but wonder if it isn't easier just to use regular framing materials and get on with my work. Do I have to offer conservation framing? Is there an easier way to sell it?

A. Yes, you should offer conservation framing — certainly for the needs of the customer, as well as to protect yourself in the event of damage to a valuable piece. There are two things you can do to lessen the need for the full explanation. One is to have a handout that explains the ways and needs of conservation. This combined with a display made of pieces that have been damaged by plywood backing, corrugated cardboard, and masking tape, will show your customer the results of poor framing.

In addition, take two pieces of rag board (cream or off–white) 8"x10," cut a mat opening in one, and attach that one to the other piece with linen tape on the inside to form a book fold. Attach a small print with Japanese hinges to the backing board. This little display piece will tell your customer a great deal. She can hold it in her hands and see the special way her artwork will be handled.

We have a frame shop and gallery in a small town. Occasionally, we get a shopper who comes in, looks around and leaves. When we talk to her she doesn't respond. I don't like letting her just walk out the door — how should I deal with this shopper?

A. This shopper is either timid, suspicious, lost, or has a language problem. None of these characteristics is reason not to pay attention to her or not to try to sell her your products. She will require different handling than a more gregarious customer. Since she is in your shop, you may as well give her the 50 cent tour. Even if she *is* lost — she may turn into a customer. Be very friendly and talkative. Don't raise your voice. If she's deaf, she'll read your lips; if she doesn't speak the language, shouting won't help. Show her around the store, pointing out areas of interest, constantly talking about what it is your shop does. Show her many items, and ask lots of questions that can be answered with a "yes" or a nod. Don't talk fast, but keep talking — the silent pauses are awkward.

If she pauses in front of anything, explain it, providing her reaction is positive (a smile is good enough), and try to sell it to her. How? Explain all of the benefits of using this service or owning this art piece, and tell her how she can pay for it — check, credit cards (be specific), on approval, lay-away, etc. — and then ask her if she wants to take it with her today. Is that too pushy for you? Well, if you wait for this woman to ask all the questions she needs to make a decision, she'll just walk out the door.

We accept two credit cards from our customers. The bank we deal with charges us 3–1/2 percent on the amount charged. Since we think the charge is high and our prices are low, we add the 3–1/2 percent to the customer's bill when they choose to pay with a credit card. Do you think this policy is OK?

A. No. This 3–1/2 percent should be buried in your pricing, just as your other expenses are. Bank charges are part of doing business and become part of the retail price of goods. Other expenses that are worked into the retail price are rent, heat, light and advertising. Each customer pays a portion of the business expenses with each purchase. Of course, you are concerned with with keeping your prices low — adding this small amount to your fitting charge or moulding will not lose a customer. You don't lose a customer for $5; you lose him because he is not treated properly and/or he does not receive the value he should.

We have a customer who was "permitted" to buy an "original replica" of Jean–Honoré Fragonard's painting *Girl Reading* by depositing $5,000 in a particular bank. It was meant as a premium, such as a toaster, but

this lady thinks she has the real thing. She has ordered a top–of–the–line frame. Should I tell her the "painting" is just a reproduction?

A. This is rich! I have had this exact experience. Our local bank "let" people buy the reproduction of a famous painting for $20 if they opened an account. The pieces are reproductions on canvas stretched on wooden bars. You may have noticed your customer's Fragonard is not square and the bars are warped — you'll have to restretch it on new bars.

The first time I encountered this type of reproduction, the customer unwrapped it and set it on the sales table. I commented on Claude Monet's style and colors, and she asked me if I knew him. Hmmm . . . so I decided to tell her what I knew about the artist and I told her that this was a nice reproduction. Whoops! She insisted that it was an oil painting. I, swimming in stupidity, showed her a "real" oil painting. She told me I didn't know what I was talking about and left the shop in a huff. And I thought truth and honestly were supposed to win every time.

Two days later, the next of these reproductions came into the shop. I commented to the owner about her fine taste in choosing such a delightful picture. I told her I was sure she would enjoy it for many years, and I especially admired her choice of an elegant frame (gold period frame with velvet liner, of course.) She was happy; I was happy. Better to err on the side of grace.

I know you feel bad because your customer is having a quality frame made for such an inexpensive article. Just think of how wonderful it will look once it is framed.

It is not your place to put a value on her picture. Each person places a value on each and every thing he or she has — it has little to do with dollar value. It has everything to do with sentiment, nostalgia, guilt, status — the item's emotional worth. Just how much would a tintype of *your* great–great–grandmother be worth to *you*? How about to a stranger?

If you suspect fraudulent selling practices, however, the police should be notified. If it's just a case of a lack of education, you might suggest that your customer visit the local museum or take a class in art appreciation.

I have read that the average frame price is on the plus side of $85. My shop is as average as they get, and the average price is $50. What am I doing wrong?

A. If you are still in business after 12 years AND you are making a satisfactory living from the business, you are not doing anything wrong. As long as sales with this average price cover your cost of goods and operating costs with a decent amount remaining as your profit, you are in great shape.

There are many price levels of products in our industry. If you have chosen to provide the customer with a low priced product and can produce it without losing money, then you have things under control; however, if you are not making money, you'd better get control fast!

Your customers come in as a result of your location, the advertising, the signage, the windows, products and services carried and displayed, the decor of the shop, the background music played, and the manner in which your employees dress and handle each customer. If you are projecting an "upscale image" with low prices, you are missing the point. Marketing is very important to your business. There are many books available on marketing for small business, including *How to Sell More Framing* available from *DECOR* magazine.

I have been in business for 14 years. What can I do to get my customers to pick up their work? The pictures are really starting to pile up. Most of them are nice things, such as family photos and stitchery. Some are limited edition prints and law–school diplomas. They take up a tremendous amount of space, and most of them couldn't be resold even if I put them up for sale. What can I do?

A. To deal with the items you have now — particularly pieces that are more than a year old — remove the moulding and glass and re–use them. Carefully wrap the artwork; create a file to hold the order forms, worksheets and descriptions of the unframed pieces. Pack all this away somewhere. We used to keep the wrapped pieces in the "attic" (the space above the dropped ceiling).

You can check state laws on the resale of the customer's goods. In some states, you can sell the pieces; in others, you can't. Don't bother posting signs that say "Not responsible for goods left for more than 30 days," because the statement isn't true. You are still responsible.

To stop this practice from continuing, take a deposit for each frame job. Better yet, have the customers pay in full. "Oh," you might think, "how could I suggest such a thing to my good customers?" Easy. After you have written up the order, say, "Would you like to pay for this now — or leave a deposit?" If customers say they've never had to do this before, lean over and whisper "Well, our choice is getting a deposit or raising our prices."

Another way to encourage customers to pick up framed pieces is to get the jobs done quickly while interest is high. How quickly? A day, a week — never more than two weeks. Also, make it clear when each order will be ready, and say that you won't call unless you have a question about the project.

If you have the frame ready by Tuesday and the customer hasn't picked it up by Wednesday, call her and tell her it's ready and it looks wonderful. Don't let those pieces stand around! The situation will only get worse, and you will be a collector of unwanted goods.

We are custom framers who routinely visit customers at home and at work, bringing moulding corner samples with us. Currently, we put the metals in one long box and the woods in another. This method is very time–consuming and disorganized and does little to properly display the samples. Do you know where I could find a portfolio or portable case that could store mouldings the way they are displayed on a shop wall? They should be easily shown to the potential customer and must look professional.

A. Two ordinary sample/catalog cases should handle your mouldings and mat corners. These are sold in most luggage departments and at office supply stores. To customize, cut pieces of black–core suede–covered mat board to fit each case. Then stick small pieces of hook–and–loop fabric to the boards and to the backs of the mouldings. The boards will look like the ones moulding salesmen use.

Two rows of mouldings will fit on each board. Three or four boards will fit into each case. Surely you can do business with 50 select mouldings. You can change the mouldings to suit different customers. Do you also carry mat board samples? Get a set of swatch books from your suppliers. Or use the standard corners, but take only 100 of your favorites. Those are the only ones you are going to sell, anyway.

Even though my shop walls are hung with samples of creatively framed pieces, my salespeople never seem to sell them. I swear my people find the least–expensive way to do a job, and I cannot get them to upgrade

their sales. I would like to increase the price of the average frame job — and I'd like to make sure customers see what we can do.

A. The problem here may be that your salespeople don't really perceive the value of custom framing. They need to understand that framing decorates the piece to be framed, in addition to protecting and presenting it.

Perhaps your employees live on an economic level that does not permit them to spend money on custom framing. If so, they may not understand why anyone would spend "that kind of money" to simply hang up a piece when all they really need is four thumbtacks!

Framing serves many people differently. One person may consider a frame "just a holder" for his certificate, while another looks upon a frame as an fine piece of furniture. Customers bring in items that have sentimental, decorative or investment value. The actual worth of these items varies with each customer and has little bearing on the price paid.

Your salespeople may tell you that customers often request the least costly frame. Explain that a customer might make such a request because she doesn't know how much custom framing costs.

More than anything, your employees need to understand that when a customer says she wants a plain black frame or the least–expensive frame, what she really wants is to learn the base price, so she can work from there.

So how do you motivate your salespeople to upgrade framing sales?

1. Set up meetings with all employees, and discuss the needs of different customers as well as the importance of doing the best job possible. Explain how disappointed customers will be if they are only offered one framing choice.

2. Sponsor a framing contest among your framers and designers. Have customers vote for the winner.

3. Pay a commission, perhaps 1 or 2 percent of sales above a certain quota. The quota can be the break–even level for the store. Pay the commission every two to four weeks. The more often it is paid, the more it works as an incentive.

Let's say you have an antique charcoal drawing in a 23–karat gold frame with brilliant French matting, and a customer comes in and touches it and drops it. What should you do?

A. This is a policy question. Should you make the customer pay for it? We're not talking about thousands of dollars here, we're talking about a few hundred bucks, maybe. I'd say take the loss.

If the customer says "Oh, I am so, so sorry. Oh, oh, can I pay for it, please? I insist." I'd say "Of course you can. Let me fix it up and make it so that it looks wonderful hanging on your wall." But if she doesn't offer to pay, then I would not force her. In fact by being incredibly understanding and taking all the blame yourself she will feel incredibly guilty. She will think you are wonderful and end up buying something anyway.

As a retailer I feel that I'm going to take some losses either through theft or breakage, and that's just part of the game.

LOCATION

My gallery is located in a small town, population 10,000. We are presently in a rented building. Business is okay, but not great. I own property along a major highway 14 miles from town. I plan to buy a building there to house a gallery. Would this be a smart move?

A. Location is very, very important. Every city is different. Each has its traffic patterns, and each community has its shopping habits. Traditionally, shopping on a regular basis is done within four miles of home. Your ability to bring along your present customers would be most important. Fourteen miles is a long distance. A major highway? Can and will people stop? Before making a move, be sure you have considered your community's buying habits and traffic patterns, parking, location of competitors, distance of your location from housing, and the trading area.

We have been in the same location for six years. We will be moving to a strip shopping center in a few months. Presently, our hours are Tuesday through Saturday, 10 a.m. to 5:30 p.m. We close early on Saturday during the summer. Since our customers are accustomed to these hours, should we continue with them or go along with the hours of shops in the center?

A. Definitely keep the same hours as the shopping center. You may have trained your old customers, but you should be getting new customers because of your new location. One reason for being in a shopping center is to benefit from the traffic of other businesses. Shoppers may not know the hours each store keeps, but they are aware that a specific shopping center is open on specific days and evenings.

They will be disappointed if you're closed when other shops are open. You mentioned closing Monday and early on Saturday: this is very risky.

Unless the entire shopping center is closed on Monday, you should be open all day, as well as staying open on Saturday afternoon. If these days are particularly slow for you, reduce your staff to the minimum, and use this time to catch up on other work, such as inventory and ordering.

The most important point is that shopping hours must be convenient for your potential customer. You should be open the hours a customer expects.

We have been at our present location for four years. Our space is too small — only 675 square feet. Two locations have become available in the area. One is the second floor above a beauty salon that has been in business for 15 years. The second is an old house with lots of character and parking space, but it is just a bit beyond the business center. Both have 1,000 plus square feet. Which do you think is a better choice for a frame shop with a limited amount of art?

A. The location of your shop is the most important business decision you will make. The location determines the clientele, which in turn determines the type of products (framing and art) you will carry. Assuming that both of these locations still will serve your present clientele, we can look at the characteristics of each space.

First consider the space over the beauty salon. Will your customers walk up the stairs to get to you? You are asking a lot for them to do that. A first–floor location always will do more business than one on the second floor, even if you have an elevator. Besides the physical aspects of walking up the stairs, you also have a psychological problem of a customer walking into an unknown (unseen from below) place and wondering if a salesperson up there is just waiting to pounce on him. The good side to a second–floor location is that the customers who do come up will be "qualified buyers." Second–floor locations are common in metropolitan cities but still restrict sales, compared with sales potential in a first–floor space at the same location.

Another concern I have is the proximity of the beauty salon. Yes, it will have regular customers who may become customers of yours. But what about the odors that are present? Have you ever experienced the smell of a "permanent "? It takes a long time for that odor to dissipate. Also, have you asked yourself about getting your length moulding stock, glass and mat boards up those stairs?

The second location choice is a character–filled old house with parking.

I like the parking. The house is OK, if it can be used without expensive reconstruction, but utility bills probably will be high. The most important factor is the location being "a bit beyond the business center." Will you still have vehicle traffic? Foot traffic? Can the "house" easily be identified as a business? Will people be able to find you? Is it well–lighted? Can you benefit from any nearby landmark or shopping attraction? Will you have to drum up all your own customers?

Location hunting is difficult, but try not to get caught up in the emotional aspects. Choose a location to serve your customers in the best manner possible. Make it as easy as you can for your customers to do business with you.

Advertising

Does anyone else in the retail art business experience a drastic drop in business from May to mid–August? What do they do about it?

A. According to a survey done by the Professional Picture Framers Association, that four–month period usually represents 32 1/3 percent of the year's gross sales. The slowest month of the year is January and the heaviest is December.

To improve business during slow times, get busy. Create promotions and special sales to spark an interest in your customers. Give them a good reason to come in and spend money.

Is it better to hand address show invitations and direct mail pieces as opposed to using mailing labels?

A. The answer is YES! I think about how I react to mail when it comes to my home or business. I pick up the pack of mail and flip through it. I take out anything that looks like it's really personal — handwritten by a real human being. There is so much excitement as you start opening those envelopes first, especially if there's no clue as to the sender. It might be a letter from a customer giving me a glowing report on how she was handled in the shop. The one thing I'm sure of — it's for *me* personally.

Sometimes it's an invitation to a gallery opening, and I'm sure I've been singled out and sent a personal, handwritten invitation because I'm so important. Surely they haven't sent out a lot of these!

We use a lot of direct mail in my gallery, and my sales people have writer's cramp four times a year when we send special invitations to 3,000 of our closest friends.

We place small ads in the community newspaper. What should we put in the ads?

A. Assuming you use small ads because your advertising budget is small and you do not have money to waste — small ads or otherwise should work for you. Along with the name, complete address, phone number and business hours of your shop, all ads should include:

· An objective — what you expect from this ad

· An appeal to the target audience

· A customer benefit — why anyone should respond to ad

· A personality — through graphics and copy; even the tiniest ads have a museum, middle–of–the–road or art city personality.

I have been reading the articles in *DECOR* about the use of direct mail to advertise and promote the art and framing business. Where do I come up with names and addresses to mail to?

A. Direct mail is a very good method of reaching a target market. What type of clientele do you have presently? What type do you want? Your target market depends on your location (who can get to you), your product (who would want this product), and price (who will pay this price). These are very basic considerations, but by pinpointing your market, you will find it easier to advertise directly to them. Some ideas for gathering addresses are:

· Take names and addresses from every check, charge ticket and work order.

· Have a "guest book" for people to sign.

· Use the city directory at your main library. Look up the streets that are your most likely market, and take the addresses and names from the list.

· Trade mailing lists with a store that has similar customers but offers a different product or service, such as women's clothing, alterations, cards or gifts, flowers and arrangements, or photography.

· Buy a mailing list from a company that can supply you with a special list according to your needs. Mail list companies advertise in the Yellow Pages and are also listed in Standard and Poor's Mail List Data, available in your main library. Mailing lists can be purchased for $50 to $100 per thousand names. Lists are available by location, income, occupation, etc.

I opened my shop 10 months ago. I cannot believe how many requests for donations I have received. Every bazaar, club and organization has asked for an item to be donated. I suppose it is good advertising and community relations, but I can't afford to say "yes" to them all. Can I afford to say "no" and offend these groups?

A. You are not alone with this problem. Galleries and framers are constantly asked to give door prizes and the like, all for good causes. After many years of giving framed artwork and mirrors, we have finally gone to gift certificates. Gift certificates with a value of $25 to $50 look valuable and will be used by the customer. The best part about a gift certificate is you get to meet the recipient and possibly make a new customer.

When you give a framed piece, you do not get to meet the person receiving it. You don't know if she likes it, or if it will end up in a garage sale. With a gift certificate, you meet the customer and present your store and products. The customer leaves with something she likes.

I do not put any restrictions on the gift certificates other that a one–year expiration date. If the customer comes in and chooses a ready–made photo frame for $25 and leaves, at least she's happy. Oh, you don't want her to choose a low–margin product? Or something that just came in? Do you want a satisfied customer or not? The purpose of the "gift" is to get good customers and good relations with organizations. Don't put too low a value on the gift certificate, or it will not be redeemed.

We usually place ads in the local community paper and the Yellow Pages. Once in a while, we take an ad in support of some organization. We design and write the ads ourselves. Is there some kind of basic list of things that should be included in each ad?

A. If possible, use the "rule of thirds": one–third headline, one–third product photo and one–third copy. Aside from the layout, every ad you produce should have the name of the shop, the complete address with ZIP code and locators such as "across from Summit Mall," a phone number with area code, hours of operation, and identification of main product or product lines. Whatever copy you use in the ad should include a benefit to the customer (*why* they should buy your product) and ask them to respond ("stop in, come and see us,"etc.) This may seem obvious, but in my 22 years of placing ads, I have missed the obvious several times.

The style of the ad will give customers some clue about the type of shop you have. Look over other ads in the Yellow Pages, and note how quickly you make a judgment about the business the ad represents — expensive, bargain barn, reliable, honest, contemporary, etc. Remember, the entire purpose of placing an ad is to convince a reasonable prospect to try your product. A reasonable prospect is one who has a need, can reach your shopping area and is willing to pay for the product.

It has been suggested that I plan my advertising dollars on a monthly basis. Which, in your opinion, are the strongest months for promoting limited edition reproductions?

A. Aside from the holiday season, the best months will be those in which you plan any promotion. You can tie your promotions to regional celebrations, sporting events, civic and social happenings, or museum openings.

Regardless of the kind, you must have promotions. Note the large department stores — they have a promotion of some kind every week. It's not *what* you sell, it's *how* you sell it!

How would you price merchandise if you were having a fire sale?

A. I've never had that opportunity, but I've thought about it a number of times. I would have a sale if I had any decent goods left over, and I would also take the opportunity to buy some new goods to put with the sale to get the most mileage out of it. If you have ever gone to a close–out sale, you've seen how the owners suddenly have twice as much merchandise as they did before. That's because they called the manufacturers and asked what they had to get rid of. Plenty of manufacturers have leftover things they will give you on consignment or at low prices so that you can pad the inventory and really make the advertising work on a sale like this. If you are concerned about quality, just stand by a printed one–year guarantee saying the product stands up to your normal standards. I'd think that it would be difficult to sell custom framing under fire–sale conditions. Maybe you could have everybody dress in white jackets and gloves to show everything is nice and clean now. It might promote a certain image.

CORPORATE SALES

How do you make a presentation to designers? Do you give them discounts? What percentage of sales goes to the artists?

A. Designers who are working with an architect on a project will have made most of the decisions regarding color, size, and style. You will meet with them a couple of times to get a feel for what they want. Whatever you can pull together for your portfolio should be coordinated to suit the project. If you are presenting very specific pieces, you may use a perspective drawing of the rooms with the artwork in place. Moulding can be attached on a color–coordinated board. Remember, designers are very style conscious. Your presentation should be color–coordinated, neat, and clean.

As for discounts, my feeling is "no" with big accounts. The company the designer works for may be given a discount if it pays the bill quickly. Corporate purchases are usually made within a budget. Corporate prices are based on the total job, not the regular retail prices.

Regular decorators who bring in customers' work to be framed are given a discount — providing they pay their bills quickly. We do not handle "kickbacks" to decorators or purchasing agents. *Dealing may be hazardous to your wealth!*

And, finally, to answer your question on percentages to artists: if this is a commissioned piece, the artist will have a price. An amount is added to that price to cover operating costs and a profit. The artist may receive 30% to 70% of the selling price — it depends on other work involved.

Do you offer discounts to designers and design firms?

A. The problem of discounting has plagued our industry for decades and will continue to do so. Designers who bring you business that normally would not have been yours should be rewarded. How this reward is handled is a problem.

Most shops give designers a discount of 10 to 20 percent off the regular retail price. This gesture is a very noble one if your pricing structure is built to accommodate it. If you don't have an extra 20 percent to give away, then all you are doing is exchanging dollars. It looks good while you are doing it, but there is no profit in the transaction. All too often, the "designers" are one–time hits; they are not repeat customers.

The other problem is the timeliness of payment. If you give 20 percent and then must wait 90 days for payment, you have gone from trading dollars to losing money. Designers can be a good source of sales but must be handled firmly. Besides collecting and making sure you have built–in profit, you also will want to encourage this person to bring you customers you would not have had access to under normal business conditions.

I wish I had a quick and easy answer to the discounting problem. One solution that has been gaining favor in the industry is a rebate. After the designer has sold a certain dollar value of goods within a three–month period, she receives a rebate — or, more correctly, a credit — to her account. For example, if a designer sells $2,000 worth of art and framing within a three–month period, you will credit 20 percent, or $400 to her account. During the next three–month period, if she sells $1,600 worth of goods, the credit reduces the bill to $1,200. The credit for the second three–month period is figured on the net amount due. A 20 percent credit on the $1,200 would be $240, applicable during the next selling period, and so on. I like this method. It encourages repeat sales and keeps the relationship going, while discouraging the "one–time designer."

How does one get a mailing list for commercial accounts and for retail customers?

A. For the commercial customers, compile the list by using:

1. The regular Yellow Pages of the phone book.
2. New phone books of "Business to Business".
3. The chamber of commerce (it may have a person's name, also).
4. Industrial directories that list businesses in industrial parkways.
5. Business clubs that you join (connections are very important).

For lists of retail customers, you might:

1. Buy or trade a list from another store with similar customers but

carrying a different product (i.e., women's dress shop or a gift store).
2. Take names from each custom order, check and charge card purchase.
3. Use the phone book.
4. Use city directories available at the library.
5. Buy a list from a mail–list company (check the Yellow Pages).
6. Join clubs and use the membership lists.

If I hire someone to sell outside the shop — to call on accounts — can I just pay that salesperson a percentage of the sale and not put him or her on payroll?

A. Yes. If the person you hire sells outside of the main retail store, you can pay a "commission only, on a contract basis." What that means is that you pay that person a straight commission. The salesperson pays all the taxes. At the end of the year, you fill out form *MISC 1099* and send one to the Internal Revenue Service and one to the salesperson. The form reports the amount you have paid the salesperson.

Outside selling is not merely a delivery service or public relations service. The salesperson should bring in sales dollars that would not have been yours without the salesperson calling on or selling to the customer. That's how you justify the percentage that you pay out.

We are considering hiring a person to sell commercial accounts. How do we pay her — commission, regular hourly wage, or salary?

A. You could do any of the three you mention, or you could combine two methods by giving the person a base salary with a commission. Perhaps the commission would start after the salesperson reaches a certain quota.

I pay straight commission, which is paid in full to the salesperson without any taxes taken out. She is an independent worker and will pay her own taxes directly to the government. At the end of the year, I will file a *1099* that reports to the government the amount paid to anyone who is not in our employ.

If the salesperson also works in the shop at an hourly wage, she or he will have to be treated as a regular employee regarding payment of taxes.

I have heard speakers refer to a capability brochure. What is it, and do I need one?

A. A capability brochure is a printed folder that is used in commercial sales. Its aim is to convince clients of your capability. The brochure might have photos of framed artwork you have installed in offices or perhaps photos of your shop or building. It should have a list of your past clients and, of course, your name, location and a "personal statement" about commercial art or your shop's successes. DECOR magazine often shows specific examples of capability brochures and articles on corporate selling.

Even if you do not do "commercial" framing, you may want a brochure for residential clients. You could hand the brochures out to your customers when they visit your shop, mail them or use them as handouts at business and civic meetings.

I just lost a bid on 208 black frames. The company asked for a polished black moulding with a gold lip. I think I'm giving them a good price, yet this the third bid I've lost. What am I doing wrong?

A. Since I don't have all the details, I'll give you an idea for what has helped me in bidding for jobs.

Often the person buying framing for the company will not have any knowledge of framing. A black and gold moulding is just an ordinary piece of wood to this person. He does not realize there are so many profiles and qualities of finish. When I'm up against this situation, I will take several 3" samples of black and gold mouldings and glue them to a 8x10" piece of mat board and number each one. On the same board, I will describe each of the mouldings to explain why they are priced in that manner. With this method the buyer can see the difference, and you can justify the price.

I have a large commercial job (14 pieces) that must be shipped several hundred miles. How do I oversee transportation and installation of such a large scale job at this kind of distance?

A. Proper packing is very important. You may be able to contact a local trucking company or moving company to suggest methods of packing the pieces you have. They probably will be shipped best by truck, and the packing must be acceptable to the trucking company. Packing is a lot more than stuffing and string. There are methods to support the piece in the center of a corrugated box. Since corrugated cardboard is available in several strengths, the size and weight of the pieces will determine the proper strength of the box. For very large and heavy pieces, a crate may have to be built. Crates can be made from wood braces in combination with newsboard and corrugated cardboard.

The installation of the pieces may be handled by your company or by the company that purchased them. Obviously, if it is you, you will need to be there to do the job. What does installation mean? Will you be putting hangers in the wall or just giving instructions as to the placement? I think that a maintenance department should take the responsibility for the physical hanging, and I am always glad to suggest placement either in person or through illustrations. The company might have a designer who will do that job.

If you do get involved with the packing and the hanging, make sure you have charged for these services in your pricing; do not include these at no extra charge. These expenses could exceed the retail price of the product.

Do you have commercial jobs out of state? If so, how do you handle repairs or mistakes?

A. Yes, I have done commercial jobs out of state. Mistakes are best handled by anticipating what could happen to any piece by being shipped, unpacked, hung or looked at. Most art is framed in the most "permanent manner possible." That means we dry mount the art to foam–centered board that is cut the full size of the frame; all mats are cut full–size, and the frames are packed — no spring clips or pressure clips of any kind. Also, we seldom use wire, preferring some form of security hanger or direct wall mount.

If a problem does occur, I locate a picture framer in the area of the installation and have him or her take care of it, and I pay them to do so.

The reason we don't use spring clips is that the amount of pressure they exert from the back will force backing and mat boards to bow out at the center of the back.

The reason we dry mount the art is to keep it from wrinkling or slipping. Of course, this method is used for decorative art only. Valuable artwork is handled with conservation procedures.

We are about to hire an outside salesperson to call on commercial accounts. Should we hire a salesperson with an art background or an artist who likes to sell?

A. I would hire a salesperson with previous experience in outside sales. For example, a person who has worked as a real estate or insurance agent has had training that adapts well to this type of selling. It takes guts to call an account. You may have luck hiring someone who has sold things such as vacuum cleaners or cosmetics door–to–door. People who come from other "selling" industries have been through a training program and have an understanding of how to get and keep accounts. You can teach any good salesperson enough about artwork and framing to be an effective salesperson. My main concern would be the personality and the image the person would project for my shop.

What type of pictures should I recommend for a hospital job?

A. There are a number of determining factors. The price range of the art will be set by the client's budget. In terms of size, each piece should be large enough to stand on its own on a large wall — so it should be at least 20"x 24".

The colors should be pleasant, clean, clear and bright — not dull and depressing, but not neon. The subject matter should be chosen to suit each ward. Children's wards may present the most difficult challenge because a pleasant environment for a 3–year–old may be different than a pleasant environment for a 13–year–old.

Generally, in adult wards, impressionistic and realistic pictures of flowers, seascapes, landscapes, and even cityscapes are suitable. Portraits, however, are to be avoided. Two hospitals I dealt with did not want pictures of people (children or adults) or pets because these may upset or offend patients and visitors.

The hospital administration should give you some additional guidelines. You may also get a chance to provide artwork for certain hospital officers and doctors. We had a few doctors request abstracts, opera posters, trains and clowns.

In terms of framing, metal is a good choice because it usually will stand up well to the cleaning necessary in a hospital. If you use Plexiglas™

glazing, remember to tell the maintenance department to use the correct cleaning materials and methods.

For commercial framing jobs, is there a standard or average discount?

A. No. A common practice is to give decorators, architects or commercial companies a 15 percent or 20 percent discount — although they'll ask you for 40 percent!

The key to this answer is discount *off what*? If it's off your regular retail price, you're in the mission business, because there's no way you can give somebody 20 percent off your retail price, unless you have no operating expenses at all.

My operating expenses would more than cut into that 20 percent, and I would not be able to give it to any company unless I had compensated for it by buying the product at a better price, in volume. If you're selling 800 same size and style pieces to a hotel, then you work it out strictly volume pricing.

If the job is for 75 different pieces, each custom made without duplication, you look at exactly how much each piece costs you to turn out — time and materials — and you mark it up for your own profit plus the selling commission for whoever did the selling — the decorator or the architect or whomever. Then you go in with the price.

A framed poster that might go for $89 in the store may have a ticket of $130 for a corporate account, to compensate for the discounts and a salesperson servicing the account. In the retail situation you stand there with your product and the customer comes to you. In the corporate situation you bring your goods to them — this represents lots more work.

FINANCE

My shop did $150,000 in gross sales last year. I have applied twice to the bank for a loan and have been twice turned down. Why?

A. To answer the question, there's a lot of information I would need from you. Did you ask the *bank* why? If you haven't, call and ask. Meanwhile I'll give you a bit of information on how banks analyze a loan. This is what they look for:

Borrower Integrity – A bank lends money expecting to get it back. Loan defaults are very expensive for the bank. A judgment will be made on your character or willingness to pay. That's why it's so important for you to maintain a friendship with the banker.

Intended Use Of Loan Proceeds – Is it for stock? Improvements? To pay old bills? A bank is most likely to lend money for something that is directly profit–producing, for example, stock.

Repayment Prospects – A bank must be reasonably certain of repayment before any loan request is approved.

Some reasons why loans get rejected include:

1. Poor credit evaluation.
2. Inferior earnings record.
3. Questionable managerial talent.
4. Insufficient collateral.
5. Poor or nonexistent credit history.
6. Inconsistency with the bank's loan policy.
7. Duration of loan is too long.
8. No established relationship with the bank.
9. The bank doesn't handle this type of loan.
10. The bank's portfolio (total collection of loans) already has enough of the type of loan you requested.

Should our business be using more than one bank?

A. The bank we choose to do business with is often the one that is most conveniently located or the one we've done our personal banking with; however, your choice of banks should be based on the bank's ability to serve your needs. What do you need from them? Some things to think about when selecting a bank include: checking accounts, interest bearing checking accounts, locations, night deposits, credit lines, processing charge card sales, and equipment leases.

Banks have had to change their style of operation in the past five years. They are openly competing with each other for business. Even though frame shops are "small" businesses, they will generate enough cash and service charges to make it worthwhile for a bank to want their business. Not all banks are geared to servicing business, some service residential needs or savings and loans/mortgages. You can call and ask to see a bank officer to handle your business, or you can go into the bank and ask to meet with someone to discuss the bank's suitability. If you are doing $100,000 a year in sales, you will be of interest to the bank. Shop around and compare services. If you can find one bank that can fill most of your needs, that's the one to do business with. One bank is easier to deal with than two — and only one checkbook to balance!

I went to a bank for a loan. A request for a list of my assets made me realize how little I have in inventory and equipment. Is this normal? By the way, I did not get the loan.

A. Bankers are looking for more than just inventory and equipment. They are looking for tangible and intangible assets. The entire loan process is complicated, but I can tell you this: NEVER go to the bank without a complete business plan. Within the plan, you will list your assets. These may include:

TANGIBLE ASSETS

A. Personal Assets

B. Business Assets

C. Location

D. Product

E. Services

INTANGIBLE ASSETS

A. Credit Rating

B. Experience
C. Honesty
D. Character
E. Pioneering
F. Saturation Of Market

Look at your presentation as if you are the bank representative. Ask yourself this question: would I lend me money?

I have been operating a frame shop for seven years, and my gross sales have just hit $200,000. I am planning to open a gallery next fall, and I figure I will need start–up money. How do I go about getting a loan from the Small Business Administration? Do I have to be turned down by two banks first?

A. No, you don't have to be turned down by two banks. There are several types of loan programs available through SBA. The availability of direct loans is very limited and will take a great deal of time and government paper–shuffling. But there are other options.

In the past, I have used the 7(a) program, under which the SBA primarily provides eligible small businesses with a loan guarantee. Loans used for new construction, the rehabilitation of real estate, the purchase of machinery and equipment, and working capital may be eligible for such a guarantee.

Financing is secured through a private lending institution, while the SBA guarantees up to 90 percent of the loan. That means the bank will only take a 10 percent risk, a percentage that appeals to most banking institutions. The guaranteed amount may not exceed $500,000. The loan also will have a controlled interest rate and time period.

The SBA will expect you to fill out the forms yourself. In this way, you will display your knowledge of the business side of your retail operation. You also will need a full business plan to get this loan. Outlines of business plans are available from SBA and are included in many business books.

To receive a copy of the loan package, call your local SBA office (under government listings in the phone book), and request one. The local chapter of SCORE (Service Corps of Retired Executives) will also have these loan packages, as will any bank that is approved for this type of loan. Since this loan is based on bank approval, it usually is processed very quickly (in a matter of weeks), depending on the bank.

Often, there are other programs available to stimulate reinvestment and job creation within a certain area of a city. Check with your local business or economic development board, which is usually part of the mayor's office.

If I borrow from a bank, can I get the prime rate?

A. Probably not. The prime rate is the normal interest rate that banks charge to their most credit worthy corporate borrowers. It is the lowest interest rate the bank charges. Like other interest rates, it is determined by supply and demand. The prime rate fluctuates with other interest rates, and these fluctuations reflect the general economic conditions.

In general, small firms — that's us — pay higher interest rates (1–3 percent over prime) than the large firms, because we fail more often and are therefore riskier.

ACCOUNTING

I want to buy a cash register. I've looked at the electronic models. How many departments would I need to run a frameshop/gallery?

A. Electronic cash registers will give you a vast amount of information. I have been using one in my frame shop and gallery for over 10 years. I'm currently using 22 departments. Each day the register records each sale within each department.

At the end of the day, when I clean out the register, I clear out the information for the day's sales which is divided into the proper departments. This information is then recorded on an accounting sheet so that when I compile the information for a complete month, I can see the strengths/weaknesses of departments and perhaps note trends within the shop. I think this is very important. I want to know how much I am selling within a department so I can make a judgment about purchasing more in that area or perhaps dropping the line altogether.

The following list contains many of the departments I have used throughout the years: fabric stretching, labor, frame restoration, glass, fitting, matting, custom wood frames, custom metal frames, ready–made wood frames, metal section packages, photo frames, dry mounting, laminating, ready–made mats, miscellaneous frame supplies, framed art, originals, show posters, loose art, decorative items, pedestals, sculptures, gift certificates and consignment goods.

Do I have to use a CPA to do my books, or could I just hire a bookkeeper or do them myself?

A. That depends on exactly what you want from these "books." A bookkeeper records all information that affects the financial condition of your business. A bookkeeper or an accountant then classifies, sorts and summarizes this information to give a condensed picture of the business. Bookkeeping, then, is the systematic recording and sorting of financial information of the business. Accounting goes beyond the summarizing. It includes the above practices — and more. Accounting also is concerned with the analysis and interpretation of financial information and with setting up the bookkeeping system.

Bookkeeping is recording; accounting is analysis. If you are capable of doing your own book work, do it. It will save you money on employment of a bookkeeper. You will also benefit by knowing what is going on at all times. If you want to learn, take a course or buy an instructional book. When your business gets to be more than you can handle, you could hire a part–time bookkeeper. Accountants should be used for analysis and advice. They usually charge more per hour than bookkeepers, so I would not want to pay them to sort out my petty cash receipts. Save the accountant for the big stuff.

I've heard several speakers refer to their operating expenses as a percentage of sales. What percentage should expense be, and how can I calculate that figure?

A. Every sales dollar received by a business is split to pay one of three types of expenses:

1. *Cost Of Goods* — art, mat board, moulding, nails, glass, etc.
2. *Operating Expenses* — rent, utilities, payroll, insurance, advertising, etc.
3. *Profit* — yes, you, too, can make a profit if you do some planning.

A shop that sells artwork as well as custom framing might allocate 40 percent of gross sales to the cost of goods, 40 percent to expenses and 20 percent to profit.

To use that allocation as a guideline, you will have to keep a close watch on your cost of goods and expenses, and you will have to reduce those costs as often as possible. If you cannot reduce your cost of goods and expenses to allow for profit, then you will have to raise your selling price to accommodate the profit.

Are you among those retailers who think they cannot raise their prices? Ask yourself about the alternatives. The only way to make a profit is to reduce your expenses and your cost of goods, or raise your prices. Or forget the profit; why not declare your company not–for–profit and call it a museum instead of a gallery? Sorry, but I do take a hard line on this subject.

In answer to your second question, regarding the calculation of a percentage, "cost" divided by gross sales equals the percentage. For example, if you want to state your rent cost as a percentage of sales, you would take the amount of rent (say $10,000), divided by the amount of gross sales (say $80,000). On the calculator, punch in 10,000; press the division sign; punch in 80,000; and press the percentage sign. The answer is 12.5 percent; that is, 12–1/2 cents of each sales dollar goes to rent.

By stating each cost as a percentage of gross sales, you can determine the ones that are out of line and take action to adjust them.

How does a business owner protect himself or herself from incompetent or insufficient information from his accountant? How do you find an accountant who will give you insight on the numbers?

A. Here's a scary thought — 50% of all accountants graduated in the bottom half of their class.

In the 27 years I've been in business, I have changed accountants several times, so I now have the guts to actually interview one. That means I go into this guy's office and sit down and find out if he knows anything about retail, because we're in the retail business. And, more complicated than that, we're also in light manufacturing, so our discounts are much different, and our markups — or margins, as the accountants would say — are much different.

Make sure she or he is familiar with retail. Ask about the types of accounts. Ask for references. Ask your banker. The accountant I've had for three years does books for another frame shop 20 miles from me. I don't really care that the other shop is that close; what's important is that the accountant actually understands how to work with frame shops.

One other thing: once you've hired an accountant, have questions for her — because if you don't have any questions, she won't volunteer any answers. You've probably noticed your accountant will say, "Here's your financial statement" and hand you a nice gray cover and a report that says at the start she isn't responsible for anything inside.

Usually, once he gives you that financial statement, you're on your own. A lot of times you don't know how to read those financial statements, so you plod through them and ask the accountant if you're doing all right and she says, "Hey; yeah, you just spent a little too much this year." So you don't buy anything for two months, and then you go right back to what you were doing before.

Ask specific questions such as: how can I improve this business? Can I take more money out of the company? What do I have to do to get this company on the right track?

Pricing

How do you feel about pricing a very difficult job that goes over budget? I find I always underbid.

A. Experience will teach you more about the time required to complete complicated jobs. Meanwhile, when you give the customer the estimate explain the possible complications that may affect the price. Call the customer at the first sign of difficulty and explain the reason for the price change.

Is there a standard percentage, i.e. 25 percent, to offer a business that displays a frame shop's items for resale (golf prints in a golf shop)? What about damage? Should I have a contract?

A. As I understand this, you are framing artwork of your choice to retail in another type of store. Therefore you will have to be prepared to sell it at a wholesale. If the store buys the goods outright, the discount would be 40 to 50 percent off the list price, which is normally suggested by the manufacturer of the goods (you). If you are putting the pieces in the shop on a consignment basis, you can expect the shop to take 25 to 40 percent of the suggested retail price established by you. Should the store wish to make more money on the art, the price could be marked higher. After all, the shop that displays your goods must make a profit to stay in business. If it did not have your product hanging on the walls, it would have something else.

If pieces are damaged while in the other shop, it should be held responsible. This should be made clear at the very beginning. You should make up an invoice with all the pieces listed and mention on it that they may be returned within 60 to 90 days (or whatever) as long as there is no damage to them. They will be billed for the damaged pieces or the work that went into making the repairs.

I've read that 20 percent of the gross sales should go to the owner. I'd like to know how that's possible unless you're not paying advertising costs or rent or supplies.

A. How much did you plan on paying yourself? If your frame shop grosses $200,000 a year — you would make $40,000. That is not a lot of money for working as hard as you'll have to and for taking the monetary risk that is involved in starting your own business.

That 20 percent should be included in the price of a frame. When you price a frame 30 percent is for cost of goods, 50 percent covers labor (including overhead and employee costs) and the remaining 20 percent should go to the owner, either as draw or salary.

If your sales volume is $100,000 or more, you should pay yourself 20 percent. Maybe you have to spend less on track lighting and start putting money into your pocket instead. If you're a typical frame shop owner, you're under capitalized the first two years. When you start to make money in the third year, you go out and buy new carpeting and track lighting — and you're right back where you were before — not paying yourself. All the money is spent. You will have to cut expenses or raise your prices.

If I just opened a store, how long should it be before I start taking that 20 percent?

A. How much money did you start out with? Do not expect to be paid in the first three months unless you were heavily capitalized to begin with. When you start out, you need enough money to put in all the fixtures, buy the proper base inventory at least three times, pay all your advertising and expenses for a couple of months and pay yourself for a year. After that, you should generate enough dollars off inventory sales to keep buying more inventory.

If you wait more than a year to pay yourself, you probably were under capitalized in the beginning, so if you're not paying yourself, you're putting hat money back into the investment. I would say that you should pay yourself *something* in the first year and if you're not making at living wage by the latter half of the second year, you may have to get a real job, elsewhere.

We are starting a custom framing business and would like some advice about pricing. We plan to build our customer base from referrals. Any advice or guidance you can offer us concerning how to price various items: i.e., mats, glass, moulding and labor, would be greatly appreciated.

A. When setting prices for your products and services, among the many factors you will consider are profit, state of the economy, stiffness of competition and the reaction of your customers. Prices should be set at a level sufficient to reimburse you for the cost of the goods and services sold, (including operating expenses) and to provide a profit. These areas are very important if you are to continue in business.

On every sale, a percentage of the price goes to pay for the goods and materials used in the product; another percentage goes to cover operating expenses — the utilities, rent, employees, etc. The last, and often the smallest, percentage goes to the owner as profit. As a business owner, you should reap financial rewards — even if you're having fun. Base your prices on facts. Take the time to figure your costs, and charge accordingly. Often, framers take the prices charged by the framer down the street, reduce them, and use the reduced prices as their own in order to be "competitive." This could be disastrous. What if that framer did the same thing when he started?

DECOR does a national survey each year and publishes the results, "Pricing for Profit," in the July issue. This survey is extensive, and more than just prices are revealed. The article and the accompanying charts will give you insight into prices which are currently being charged by existing shops and how the economy effects certain regions. Your prices must include your operating expenses, your cost of goods and a percentage for profit. Compare your figures with others in the industry to see if you are in the same ballpark. Compare — do not copy. My cost of goods and operating expenses may well be different from yours, necessitating different pricing structures. For more information on pricing, see chapter six.

We opened our frame shop and gallery just four months ago. Do we need to take MasterCard or Visa? It seems like such a hassle and it's expensive. The bank wants us to pay on a sliding scale that could cost anywhere from 2 percent to 7 percent. I don't think I can give up 7 percent of my sale to the bank.

A. Yes, you *need* to accept MasterCard and Visa. This is provided to your customer as a convenience — an easier form of payment than cash. The products you sell typically have high average prices, and customers seldom have enough cash to pay for these items, especially when the purchase is impulsive. A basic principle of retail is to make it as easy as possible for your customer to make a purchase. Convenience is very important to retail sales of art and framing. You will lose customers if you do not accept charge cards. You may not even know it — they may just leave without purchasing or not even bother to stop in at all.

You can negotiate with your bank for a better rate. Explain to the banker the average ticket price is in excess of $50 and that you will be doing a large volume. You should be able to get 2.5 percent or 3 percent without too much difficulty. If not, go to a larger bank. Not all banks like to handle charge card sales. Shop around, and compare services. Find the commercial bank that will provide you with acceptance of both bank cards. It will be the same bank that you will need when you want to borrow money for business purposes, so it is good to get the relationship going soon. The percentage you pay is simply part of the cost of doing business. Just raise your fitting charges by 50 cents, and it will make up for it. If you want to handle other charge cards such as American Express or Discover you may have to deal directly with them. Check with the PPFA — they may offer this service in your state.

INDEX

Entries are filed word–by–word. **Boldface** locators indicate sections or extensive treatment of a topic.

A

actual cost, 28, 31, 32
accountants, 7, **152–153**
accounting, 7
    terms of, 11
accounts payable, 12
accounts receivable, 12, 74, 83, 85
    department, 74
advance dating, 22
advantages of discounts, 23
advertising, 4, 46, 47, **61–68**, **135–138**
    budget, 136
    discounts, 23
    methods, 19
    options, 67
    plan, 65
    and promotion, **135–138**
American, 111
American Society of Appraisers, 111
analysis, 7
anticipation, 23
antique art, 49
appraisal, 110
approval, on, 123
architects, 145
Art Buyers Caravan, 90
artist, 107, 139
art collection, 110
Art Marketing Handbook (Goodman), 112
art publishing, 112
art supply, 22
artwork, 46, 50, 55
    leasing, **79–82**
    rental, 108
    reproduction, 127
    restoration of, 46
    returns, 38
assembly production line, 76
assets, 8, 11, 13, 14
assistance, 35
attitude of employees, **36–37**

average frame price, 129, 130
average sale, 124

B

backlog of orders, 54
back room, 41
balance sheet, 10, 11, 12, 14
bank, 21
  charges, 18
  loan, **146–148**
bankers, 10, 152
banking, 147
basic formula, 27, 28
Better Business Bureau, 67
bid, 142, 145
billboards, 67
billing, 24
blue jeans, 95
bookkeepers, 7, 9, 150
bookkeeping, 8, 11, 83
  and accounting, **7–10**
bookkeeping system, 106, 151
booklet of policies, 38
break–even, 51, 130
budget, 17, 19, 42, 61, 62
business,
  cycle, 62
  entity, 8
  failure, 17
  hours, 132
  and operating experience,113
  plan, 93, 99, 147
  transactions, 9
  year, 17
buyer discounts, 23
buying frequency, 4

C

capability brochure, 142
capital, 8, 113
cards, 52
carrying
  charge, 49
  cost, 28, 30, 32
cash, 8, 19
  in advance, 23
  discounts, 23, 84
  register, 150
census, 4
chamber of commerce, 4, 67
charge cards, 37, 157
cheap, 39
check, 109
checkbook, 41
chop, 28, 49, 50, 52, 116, 117, 120, 121
Christie's, 111
clothing, 95
clothing stores, 35
COD (cash on delivery), 29, 56, 83
college, 49
colors, 144
commercial
  accounts, 71
  framing jobs, 145
commission, 72, 110, 130, 141
communications, 65
competition, 5, 62
computer, 8, 19, 92
conservation framing, 124, 125
consignment, 154
consumer credit, 83
Continuing Education, 106
contracts, 9
  advertising, 18
  framing, 71
convenience stores, 35
corner samples, 117
corporate
  art collections, 71
  purchases,139
  sales, **136–138**, **139–145**
cost, 47,75
  of goods, 13, 151
courtesy, 35
CPAs, 91, 150
credit, 21
  card, 109, 123, 126
  department, **83–86**
  history, 85
  policies, 74, 85
  reference, 21
  terms, 74
creditors, 10

cultural awareness, 5
cumulative discount, 22
current assets, 11
current liabilities, 11
current ratio, 15
customer, 39
complaints, 38
courtesy, **36–37**
damage, 130
profile, 4
satisfaction, 4
cycle billing, 24

D

daily invoices, 9
daily sales slips, 9
damage, 155
damaged goods, 119
datings, **21–22**
debt, 9
December, 19
DECOR, 4, 110, 111, 112, 116, 118, 128, 136, 142, 156
decorative accessories, 46
decorators, 145
delegating, 42, 100
deliver, 123
departments, 19, 150
deposits, 9, 37, 128
designer, 38, 139, 140
direct mail, 67, 115, 135, 136
discount, 21, **22–23**, 24, 74, 139, 140, 145, 152, 154
deferred, 22
period, 23
displays, 4, 42, 56, 125
distributor, 21, 116, 121
donations, 68, 137
door prizes, 68
drug stores, 35
Dun and Bradstreet, 106

E

Eastern European, 111
economic conditions, 79
Economic Development Board, 149
of Ohio, 106
economic survival, **51–57**
electronic cash register, 18
emotional worth, 127
employees, 19, 36, 37, 92, 94, 99, 100
estimate, 154
equipment, 3, 11, 46, 47, 56
evaluation, 72
expansions, 47, 48, 93
expenditures, 17, 19, 52
expenses, 19
expensive, 39
experience, 66
extra dating, 22

F

February, 19
Federal Trade Commission, 24
FICA, 29
finance, **146–149**
financial condition, 9
financial statements, 9, 10, **11–16**, 51, 83, 152
first–floor location, 133
fixed assets, 11
foam center board, 125
forecast, 4
Fragonard, Jean–Honoré, 126, 127
framed prints, 106
frameland, 65
Frame–O–Rama, 92
frames, 5, 42, 54
corner displays, 116
from scraps, 42
frame shops, 3, 38, 65
framing, 19, 37
freight, 28, 32
full–time, 95
fundamental accounting equation, 12
furniture, 8
future datings, 21

G

gallery, 3, 38, **103–113**
gallery owners, 107
gift certificates, 137
Girl Reading, 126
glass, 18, 33, 50, 56
glossary of accounting terms, 11
goods and services, 3, 8
government offices, 4
gross sales, 135, 146, 148
groundwork, 5
guarantee, 77
guest book, 136

H

hanging, 143
Harvard, 65
hospital job, 144
hourly rate, 29
hours, 41
hours of shop, 36
house calls, 129
housekeeping, 36
How to Sell More Framing, 128

I

image, 4, 114, 144
income statement, 10, 11,12, 13, 14, 17
incorporate, 89
increase sales, 45
individual sales record, 72
industry surveys, 4
inflation, 19
information, 9, 11
initial investment, 9
input, 9
installation, 143
interest rates, 79
interstate trade, 24
inventory, 3, 8, 12, 19, 28, 45, 46, 47, 48, 49, 92, 111, 118, 119, 120, 122, 155
    clearance, 55
    turn, 15, 28
investment art, 71
investors, 10
invoices, 9, 18, 21, 22, 23, 84
IRS, 81, 82, 108, 141

J

job description, 72
jobs per week, 54
join frames, 42

K

keeping records, 74
kickbacks, 139

L

labor, 29, 30
    charge, 30
    rate, 29
land, 8
layaway plans, 37
Learning Center, 90
lease agreement, 80
leasing, **79–82**, 108
leasing company, 81
legal considerations, 24
Legal Handbook for Small Business (Lane), 91
length moulding, 117, 121
    inventory, 116
liabilities, 8,10,11,12,13
    and equity, 14
    long-term, 12
license, 8
license bureau, 35
limited edition, 110, 117
line of credit, 85
loan, 146, 148
location, 4, 39, 45, 46, 47, 48, 61, 66, **132–134**

M

mailing lists, 42, 136, 140
maintenance, 18
maintenance agreement, 81
management, 77, **98–100**, 113
managers, 10
manners, 35
manufacture, 21
manufacturer, 21, 23, 89
margin, 49
markdown, 120, 121
market, 3, 5, 52
marketing, 115, 118
market research, 3, 4
market share, 48
markup, 28, 29, 30, 117, 120, 152
Mastercard, 157
mat board, 31, 32, 50
Mayfield, Robert, 33
media, 61
merchandise, 9, 12
merchandising, **114–122**
methods of payment, 37
metropolitan newspapers, 68
MISC 1099, 141
Monet, Claude, 127
money, 19, 35
month–end, 24
mortality rate, 106
moulding, 49, 52, 55, 89,
  chops, 49, 116, 117, 120, 121
  cost, 30
  length, 117, 121
  scraps, 122
move, 47
moving, 45, 132
music, 37, 114, 115

N

naming a business, 90
National Art Materials Trade
  Association (NAMTA), 116
neighborhood, 48
networking, 74, 91
net worth, 8
new galleries, 106
new market, 45
new products, 45, 46
newsletter, 63
newspaper, 63, 68
New York, 46
notes payable, 12
notes receivable, 12

O

on account, 8
operations, 49
operating costs, 51, 139
operating expenses, 13, 18, 29,
  145, 151
operating ratios, 15
ordering, 42
ordering system, 54
order practices, 50
orders, 41
  and turnaround time, 120
ordinary dating, 22
organize, 9, 43, 76
original replica, 126
output, 9
outside sales, 144
overdue, 56
owners, 10
owner's equity, 8, 9, 10, 12, 13, 14
owner's pay, 155

P

packaging, 4
packing, 142, 143
Parker, William P., 16
part–time, 95
patent, 90
patronage discount, 22
payables, 17, 52
payment, 9
payouts, 9
payroll, 17, 18, 95
personality, 96
personnel, 46, 47, 50
phone, 37
photo art, 115
photo frames, 123, 124
pictures, 37

P&L, 12, 17, 18
planning, 106
    of advertising, 65
planning for growth, **45–50**
Plexiglas™, 144
policies, 38
poster, 38, 114, 115, 118, 145
present market, 48
price, 54, 107
price levels, 39
pricing, 4, **27–33**, 53, **154–157**
    formula, 28, 30, 31
    moulding, 29
    Pricing for Profit, 156
prime rate, 149
prints, framed, 106
priorities, 42
problems, 38
processing frame orders, 42
product, 5, 35, 47
product line, 45, 47
production, 12, **101–102**
Professional Photographers Association (PPA),116
Professional Picture Framers Association (PPFA), 56, 157 116, 135
profile, 5
profit, 45, 47, 48, 89, 128, 139, 151, 156
Profit and Loss Statement, 11
profitability, 85
pro forma, 21, 23
promotion, 23, 47, 107, 138
promotional pamphlets, 68
proprietorship, 8
public library, 4
public, the, 10
purchases, 18, 19
purchasing agents, 139
purchase supplies, 76

Q

quality control, 98
quantity discount, 22
questions, 37

R

radio, 68
rag board, 125
rag mat, 33
ratios, 15
ready–made, 30, 56, 119, 122, 123
rebate, 22
receipt, 9
receivables, 17
record, 9
Rembrandt, 114
rent, 55, 76
    and store space, 8
rental artwork, 108
reproductions, 127
reputation, 39
responsibilities, 100
restoration of artwork, 46
return, 38
revenue, 12, 111
risk, 155
Robinson–Patman Act, 24
rule of thumb, 19

S

salary, 18
sales, 4, 18, 19, 92, 119, 124
    in art and framing, 13
    clerk, 35, 96
    in case of fire, 138
    plan, 73
    staff, 35
    volume, 101, 155
salesperson, 71, 95
sample cases, 129
samples, 47
sample wall, 42
schedule work orders, 92
scraps, 122
sculpture, 46
seasonal dating, 22
second–floor location, 133
security hanger, 143
seen and not heard, 35
sell, 21

selling, 123, 126
on approval, 109
service, 35
Service Corps of Retired Executives (SCORE), 148
shipping, 142, 143
shopping
center, 46, 132
habits, 132
shop rate, 29
show invitations, 135
shows, 42
sign, 37
Small Business Administration (SBA), 89, 148
small business owners, 65
Sotheby's, 111
Sources Directory, 110, 116
spring clips, 143
staff, 39
statements, financial, 9, 17
stock, 47, 55
storage, 122
strategy, 3 ,47
strip shopping center, 132
summarize, 9, 11
supermarkets, 35
supervising, 41
supplier, 21, 23, 76, 89
supplies, 17, 76
system, the, 9

T

tally sheet, 18
target market, 63, 136
tax department, 122
terms, 21, 85
terms of sale, 21
time, 42, 48
time clock, 96
time management, **41–43**
time study, 101
tintype, 127
tourist, 108
trade credit, 83
trading area, 4
traffic patterns, 4, 132
training, 42, 94, 124, 144
training program, 73
transportation, 4
turnaround, 120
turnover, 49
types of jobs, 42

U

underselling, 38
united inches, 31, 32
United States, 83
Utah, 46
utilities, 18

V

value, 39, 114, 122, 124, 126, 127, 130
visa, 51, 157
volume framing, **75–78**

W

wages, 8
wall decor, 80
waste, 28, 30, 32
wholesale, 154
wholesalers, 116
windows, 42
wood moulding, 119
word–of–mouth, 5
working capital, 15
work order form, 102
work sheet, 18
Works of Art on Paper, 118

Y

yearly production, 76
yearly sales, 4
Yellow Pages, 67, 110, 137, 138, 141

APPENDIX

The articles contained in this anthology were previously published by *DECOR* magazine. Listed by chapter number and page they are:

Chp.		
1	page 3	Starting a Frame Shop or Gallery, August 1981
2	page 7	Bookkeeping & Accounting, December 1981
3	page 11	Financial Statements, January 1982
4	page 17	The Budget: A Guide to Cash Control, October 1981
5	page 21	Credit Terms from Suppliers, March 1982
6	page 27	Pricing the Custom Product, July 1982
7	page 35	Customer Service, February 1992
8	page 41	Time Management, August 1986
9	page 45	Planning for Growth, January 1986
10	page 51	Economic Survival, September 1991
11	page 61	Advertising, October 1985
12	page 65	Developing A Plan, September 1981
13	page 71	Corporate Sales, July 1982
14	page 75	Volume Framing, February 1991
15	page 79	Leasing Artwork, November 1982
16	page 83	Credit Department, May 1982
17	page 89	Questions & Answers from the *Ask The Experts* column, have appeared in various issues from 1983 to 1993.

Books referred to in *The Articles of Business*

Art Marketing Handbook
by Calvin J. Goodman, gee tee bee
Business Forms for Galleries & Frame Shops
Columba Publishing. Co.
Framer's Work Scheduling Book
by V. Kistler, Columba Publishing. Co.
Floorplans for Galleries & Frame Shops
by Strasburg & Kistler, Columba Publishing. Co.
Frameshop Worktables, Fixtures & Jigs
by Paul MacFarland CPF, Columba Publishing. Co.
Glazing: Picture Framing Glass & Plastic
by William P. Parker, CPF, Columba Publishing. Co.
How To Sell more Framing
by Debbie Karpiel Hagan, Commerce Publishing Co.
Legal Handbook for Small Business
by Marc J. Lane, AMACOM
What Every Artist & Collector Should Know About The Law
by Scott, Hodes, Dutton & Co.
Works of Art on Paper, Video
from Commerce Publishing Co.

Associations referred to in *The Articles of Business*

ASA, American Society of Appraisers
Washington, DC
NAMTA, National Art Materials Trade Association
Clifton, NJ
PPFA, Professional Picture Framers Association
Richmond, VA
PPA, Professional Photographers Association
Atlanta, GA
SBA, Small Business Administration
Washington, DC
SCORE, Service Corps of Retired Executives
Washington, DC

Books & Videos

The Library of Professional Picture Framing

Picture Framing Vol 1 by Vivian Kistler CPF, GCF

A complete overview of professional custom framing. History of Framing. Moulding. Ordering. Cutting & joining wood & metal moulding. Cutting glass & plastics. Measuring. Basic Mat Cuts. Stretching Canvas. Conservation. Work Orders. Floorplans. Use to study for the CPF test.

96pp 8½ x 11 B116 $19

Mat Cutting & Decoration Vol 2 by Vivian Kistler CPF, GCF

Inlays, offsets, doubles & 8-sided mats! Step-by-step directions for 50 different mats, basic to advanced. Measurements. Proportion. Color. Fractions. Faux Finishes. Hand-cut designs. Singles, doubles, multiple openings, scroll. V-grooves, French mats, cove & fabric-wrapped mats

96pp 8½ x 11 B019 $19

Framing Needlework & Fabric Vol 3 by Vivian Kistler CPF, GCF

12 Methods of mounting textiles. 15 Projects. Block & stretch needlepoint. Identify types of needlework & fabric before you work on them. Tools and materials, cleaning methods, repairs, pressing. Learn to frame crewel, needlepoint, cross-stitch, antique samplers, quilts, scarves, kimonos, carpets, scrolls, hankies, doilies, Persian paintings, papyrus, weavings & flags.

96pp 8½ x 11 B027 $19

Conservation Framing Vol 4 by Kistler et al

Controlling damage to art. Glazing. How to make hinges. Adhesive choices. Selecting mount and matting boards. Encapsulation, deacidification. Solutions to many problems. How papers and boards react to humidity. Storage. Projects: watercolors, papyrus, pastels, photos, and skin documents.

96 pp 8½x11 B035 $19 July 1997

Mounting Methods Vol 5 by Kistler et al

How to mount paper using wet, spray, pressure sensitives and heat activated adhesives. Selecting boards. Handling buckling. Setting up the workroom. Choosing equipment. Laminating. Canvas Transfer. Step-by-Step Projects

96pp 8½x11 B043 $19 July 1997

Framing Photography Vol 6 by Allan R. Lamb CPF

Quick identification chart. Photography time line. Early presentation techniques. Suitable framing methods for: ambrotype, daguerreotype, Ilfochrome Classics®, albumen, tintype, Polaroid®, snapshots and others. Mounting: Wet, dry, spray, and pressure-sensitives. Projects. Creative framing

96pp 8½x11 B051 $19

The Articles of Business by Vivian Kistler CPF, GCF

The business of operating a frame shop and gallery. Volume Framing, credit departments. Pricing the custom product. Employee productivity. Leasing, corporate sales. Marketing, advertising, financial statements, credit terms, and more. Over 100 answers to questions sent to the "Ask the Expert"

192pp 6x9 B280 $20

Color & Design for the Picture Framer by Nona Powers CPF

Written and designed for the picture framer by a practicing, award-winning professional picture framer. How to select the size, color and shape of mats, mouldings and decorative elements. Relationship of color to size, warm to cool color, moulding color to mat color. Full-color artwork with matting selections help you to understand framing design. Workbook included. This book is the basis for Nona's popular two-day course.

96pp 8½x11 B485 $30

How to Build Frameshop Worktables
Fixtures & Jigs by Paul MacFarland CPF

Building plans for 25 projects. Build a Frame Rack • Frame Jack • Support for Length Moulding • Spool Wire Box • Table for your Mat Cutter • Roll Storage • Bin Cart & more! Materials, Tools & Techniques. Table, tops, cabinets, clamps, storage for mat, glass, moulding & customer's goods.

64pp 8½ x 11 B361 $19

Brian Wolf's Sketchbook of Mat Designs by Brian Wolf, CPF, GCF

A replica of Brian's personal sketchbook containing his favorite flourishes & panel designs. The designs are appropriate for carving or toning with powdered colors. Directions for transfering the designs to your mats.

32pp 8½ x 11 B302 $15

Business Forms for Galleries & Frame Shops by Vivian Kistler CPF, GCF

Consignment Record & Agreement. Work Orders. Sales Records. Projected Sales Charts. Record of Condition of Artwork. Purchase Orders. Time Sheets. Tax Exempt Slips. Petty Cash Slips. Commission Forms. Proposal. Inventory. Yearly Planner. Sales Tracking & More. Ready to copy.

32pp 8½ x 11 B264 $12

Floorplans for Galleries & Frame Shops by Strasburg & Kistler

Maximize your space! 19 floorplans. Equipment. Lighting. Flooring. Storage. Safety. Front & backroom plans for shops from 400 to 4,000 sq.ft. Grid paper included, plus furniture & equipment patterns!

32pp 8½ x 11 B272 $14

How To Do Object Box Framing by Vivian Kistler, CPF, GCF

How to attach items in a shadow box. 20 different projects. Attachments, backgrounds, special requirements for problem pieces. Coins. Plates. Fossils. Animals. Ceramics. Jewelry. Flowers. Figurines. Buttons. Masks. Clothing.

32pp 8½ x 11 B345 $14

Videos

The Basics of Picture Framing
by Vivian Kistler CPF, GCF

Basic training for picture framers & designers! Step-by-step instructions. Moulding. Squaring a mat cutter. Cutting single & double mats. Color selection. Matboards. Measuring. Cutting glass. Framing needlework. Stretching paintings on canvas. Attaching artwork. Fitting: dust cover. screw eyes, wire.

60 min VHS V132 $30

Mat Cutting & Decoration
by Vivian Kistler CPF, GCF

Step-by-step instructions for cutting single, double, inlay & V-groove mats. Cutting & decorating techniques. Fabric-wrapped, shadow-box, traditional French mats, powder panels and application of marbled papers. Conservation. Attaching Artwork. Matting needlework & 3-D objects.

60 min VHS V140 $30

Conservation Framing
by Vivian Kistler CPF, GCF

How to make hinges, mix paste and support fine artwork. How to preserve newsprint and broken and brittle artwork. Understanding neutral pH. How to de-acidify & encapsulate art on paper. Selecting boards, tapes, adhesives & glazing. Hinges, flanges, mounting strips, pockets, float & sink mats. Storage.

60 min VHS V175 $30

Framing Needlework
by Vivian Kistler CPF, GCF

Block & stretch needlepoint. Frame any type of fabric or stitched piece. Types, supplies & materials. Blocking, stretching, matting & framing. Projects include sweaters, doilies, Chinese embroidery, scarves, cross-stitch, crewel & needlepoint, Persian paintings, Molas & sheer fabrics. Conservation. Lacing, pinning, stapling & sewing. A guide to color coordinating matboards with embroidery floss is included.

60 min VHS V167 $30

Color Selection in Matting
by Vivian Kistler CPF, GCF

How to handle "problems" such as black & white pictures, old photos, mixed sizes, mismatched art. See how different color mats change the mood of a picture. Color is the single most important element in a framed presentation; it affects all purchasing decisions. Learn to use color effectively.

60 min VHS V191 $30

A deck of 192 colors chips to use in conjunction with the video helps you to understand the relationship between colors; tints, tones and shades.

2x3" Deck CD1 $10

Videos

The Art of Ink Lines
by Brian Wolf CPF, GCF

Brian shows you in exacting detail the techniques of perfect lines on mats. How to draw consistent ink lines. Laying out lines. How to use lines as an accent on inlays. Drawing lines on circles and ovals. Lining offset corners. Coordinating multiple lines. How to use a ruling pen.

30 min VHS V40X $20

Painted Mat Decoration
by Brian Wolf CPF, GCF

Brian demonstrates the step-by-step process of painting faux panels. Unique recipes for marbleizing & faux finishes. Brian shows you several methods of making panels by masking, stencil, powder resist, and glazing. Gold, malachite & metallic recipes.

30 min VHS V426 $20

Hand Carved Mats
by Brian Wolf CPF, GCF

Brian demonstrates his award-winning carving skills. The tools and techniques are thoroughly explained and demonstrated. Subtle, carved designs accent mats and create an elegant balance. How to add top & bottom ornaments and partial grooves.

30 min VHS V418 $20

Decorative Transfer Borders
by Brian Wolf CPF, GCF

Brian shows you how to use dry transfer borders and design elements to create exquisite mats easily! Burnishing techniques, design planning, and short cuts. How to correct mistakes.

30 min VHS V434 $20

Marbled Paper Panels & Bevels
by Brian Wolf CPF, GCF

Learn to create extraordinary mats with marbled papers. Panels, unique corners and overlays. Bevels – thick, thin painted and wrapped. Brian uses traditional marbled papers in innovative ways!

30 min VHS V442 $20

Framing Needleart Video
by Kaye Evans, CPF

Learn an easy way to lace embroidery from a nationally certified framer and teacher of counted thread. Kaye will show how to do couching and other methods, including simple adhesive mounting of needleart. Identify and handle types of needleart including: embroidery, tatting, cross-stitch, needlepoint, crochet, Chinese stitchery & kalangas. Blocking, cleaning. Problems & solutions. Matboard and embroidery floss color guide included.

60 min VHS V205 $30

Order Form

BOOKS

The Library of Professional Picture Framing

___ Picture Framing Vol. 1	B116	$19
___ Mat Cutting & Decoration Vol. 2	B019	$19
___ Framing Needlework Vol 3	B027	$19
___ Conservation Framing Vol 4 (available 7/97)	B035	$19
___ Mounting Methods Vol 5 (available 7/97)	B043	$19
___ Framing Photography Vol 6	B051	$19
___ Articles of Business	B280	$20
___ Color & Design for the Picture Framer	B485	$30
___ How to Do Object Box Framing	B345	$14
___ Business Forms for Galleries & Frame Shops	B264	$12
___ Floorplans for Galleries & Frame Shops	B272	$14
___ Brian Wolf's Sketchbook of Mat Designs	B302	$15
___ How to Build Frameshop Worktables, Fixtures & Jigs	B361	$19

VIDEOS

___ Basic Picture Framing	V132	$30
___ Mat Cutting & Decoration	V140	$30
___ Framing Needlework	V167	$30
___ Conservation Framing	V175	$30
___ Color Selection in Matting	V191	$30
___ Optional Deck of 192 Colors	CD1	$10
___ *Set of 5 Kistler Videos*	VK5	135
___ The Art of Ink Lines	V40X	$20
___ Painted Mat Decoration	V426	$20
___ Hand Carved Mats	V418	$20
___ Decorative Transfer Borders	V434	$20
___ Marbled Paper Bevels & Panels	V442	$20
___ *Set of 5 Wolf Videos*	BW5	$90
___ Evans' Framing NeedleArt	V205	$30

Items may be ordered from a frame supply distributor
or by phone, mail or fax from:

COLUMBA PUBLISHING COMPANY, INC.
2003 W. Market St. • Akron, Ohio 44313-6917
phone 330 836-2619 800 999-7491 fax 330 836-9659

Visa & MasterCard orders may be phoned, mailed or faxed.
Mail check or money orders (US funds) with order form.

Please add $3 for shipping